Industry Influencer

Praise for *Industry Influencer*

As a former gamer who went on to own multiple million dollar companies, I know a thing or two about "leveling up." In fact, I wrote a book about it. Dr. Glenn Vo is someone who has literally leveled up by going from a successful Dentist to a leader in the Dental Industry. And his book, Industry Influencer, is the blueprint on how you can be a leader in your niche as well.

—**ERIC SIU**, author of *Leveling Up: How To Master The Game of Life* and Co-host of Marketing School Podcast

In *Industry Influencer*, Glenn Vo shares a simple plan for building authority and influence in even the most competitive industries. These principles can help anyone grow a thriving personal brand.

—**JULIE STOIAN**, JulieStoian.com

Being an influencer is much more than posting pictures and having thousands of followers. An effective influencer inspires their following and positive growth. Dr. Glenn Vo not only talks the talk but he walks the walk. Having worked with him, I have seen firsthand how he has elevated his community. *Industry Influencer* is a book that every entrepreneur should own if they are serious about being a leader in their profession.

—**MARK LACK**, branding coach for Shorten the Gap and host of Business Rockstars

There's a difference between being an "influencer" and being an "industry influencer." An industry influencer uplifts an entire profession and makes their colleagues better. Dr. Glenn Vo has done that for dentistry, and he'll help you do that in your industry.

—**DR. SHAWN DILL**, founder of Black Diamond Club and The Specific Chiropractic Centers, ShawnDill.com

Glenn Vo is a master at growing your influence online. If you follow the steps he teaches in *Industry Influencer*, you will be well on your way to making a positive impact on your industry too.

—**CHRIS TUFF**, national best-selling author of *The Millennial Whisperer* and *Save Your Asks,* ChrisTuff.me

Glenn Vo is one of the most knowledgeable online marketing experts in the dental industry. He knows how to help people make a true impact on themselves, their relationships, and their communities through a mindful, forgiving approach. His strategies not only work, but they are simple and take just a few moments of our sacred personal time to implement.

—**TOMMY BREEDLOVE**, *Wall Street Journal* best-selling author of *Legendary: A Simple Playbook for Building and Living a Legendary Life, and Being Remembered as a Legend* TommyBreedlove.com

In a world swarming with self-proclaimed influencers, Glenn Vo is the real deal. Who else is a practicing industry professional who also has a group of over 30,000 in his industry? If you want to make the leap from doctor to being well-known in your community and in an area you care about, there is no better road map than *Industry Influencer*.

This program helps you map out your WHY, so you can then build your personal brand on this framework. The content creation phase helps you publish your book, fill out your social media presence, and your website. And amplification is how you get eyeballs on your content, building relationships and speaking opportunities.

Glenn practices what he preaches, so he's showing you a step-by-step formula that you can follow to become well-known in your city and for the causes you care about.

—**DENNIS YU**, CEO, BlitzMetrics

Glenn Vo knows what it takes to build influence within an industry. Using the simple system outlined in *Industry Influencer*, anybody can build a following and become an influential thought leader.

—**ELIJAH DESMOND**, motivational speaker, emcee, author, serial entrepreneur, ElijahDesmond.com

Dr. Glenn Vo is the go-to expert on what it takes to build a thriving online brand. His strategies have helped many people use their passion and expertise to impact their industry in a positive way.

—**DR. ANISSA HOLMES**, author of *Delivering WOW: How Dentists Can Build a Fascinating Brand and Achieve More While Working Less*, DeliveringWow.com

If you're looking to build your influence and improve your status in an industry, I know of no better guide than Glenn Vo. His systems are as simple as they are effective. And they lead with integrity, building mutually beneficial relationships that position everyone involved for success.

—**DR. LEN TAU**, *The Reviews Doctor* and author of *Raving Patients: The Definitive Guide To Using Reputation Marketing To Attract Hundreds Of New Patients,* DrLenTau.com

INDUSTRY INFLUENCER

Growing Your Brand through Meaningful Connections and Engagement Online

DR. GLENN VO

NEW YORK

LONDON • NASHVILLE • MELBOURNE • VANCOUVER

INDUSTRY INFLUENCER

Growing Your Brand Through Meaningful Connections
and Engagement Online

Published in New York, New York, by Morgan James Publishing. Morgan James is a trademark of Morgan James, LLC. www.MorganJamesPublishing.com

Proudly distributed by Ingram Publisher Services.

A **FREE** ebook edition is available for you
or a friend with the purchase of this print book.

CLEARLY SIGN YOUR NAME ABOVE

Instructions to claim your free ebook edition:
1. Visit MorganJamesBOGO.com
2. Sign your name CLEARLY in the space above
3. Complete the form and submit a photo of this entire page
4. You or your friend can download the ebook to your preferred device

ISBN 9781631954818 paperback
ISBN 9781631954825 ebook
Library of Congress Control Number:
2021930048

Cover Design by:
Christopher Kirk
www.GFSstudio.com

Interior Design by:
Chris Treccani
www.3dogcreative.net

Morgan James is a proud partner of Habitat for Humanity Peninsula
and Greater Williamsburg. Partners in building since 2006.

Get involved today! Visit MorganJamesPublishing.com/giving-back

Dedication

For my wife, whom I adoringly call "Squeaky."
For my daughter, whom I lovingly call "Princess."
And for my son, whom I affectionately call "Boy."

Table of Contents

Foreword

Today we have so many options for social media connections. Facebook, Instagram, LinkedIn, Twitter, Pinterest, and many more. And any intelligent businessperson will be utilizing these to leverage their influence. But there is an underlying principle that bypasses these readily available "tools." And that is the power of connecting with other people.

I started building my brand before we had podcasts, blogs, Zoom, Skype, or any of the tools mentioned above. But the door has always been wide open for creating meaningful and productive connections with other influencers.

In *Industry Influencer*, you are about to see the very best methods you can use right now to dramatically expand your voice and reach.

Let's step back a few years to underscore that basic underlying principle. In September of 1988, I sold a health and fitness center at public auction. After three frustrating years, I had decided to just cash out and move on to the next idea. And yes, I thought I'd cash out and be set to fund my next entrepreneurial idea. Instead, I ended that day with the stark realization that I was absolutely broke and owed over $430,000 to creditors, including the non-friendly IRS.

My education in business up to that point had come from selling Christmas cards as a kid, washing neighbors' cars, and selling advertising door to door. With this enormous debt to repay, I realized I needed to learn better practices—and fast. Living in Nashville, Tennessee, I saw that there were numerous "success" conferences that showed up repeatedly. These conferences were promoted as a way to learn from the Masters of Achievement, by hearing their motivational speeches and getting their products.

Only one small problem. I was deeply in debt and could afford neither the tickets nor the products. So I simply reached out to these big names and told them my wife and I would be happy to help them at these events. We'd show up at the conference and work their tables, promoting their wonderful products to the attendees. I can't remember ever being turned down. We worked with Zig Ziglar, Brian Tracy, Tom Hopkins, Wayne Dyer, Mark Victor Hansen, Jack Canfield, and more. In serving these giants well, we got free access to the events and were given free products because of the way we generated sales. We developed personal relationships with these influencers, including getting access to their audiences and sharing the stage at their events.

Those relationships continue to open doors of opportunity. Our attitude of serving well with Zig Ziglar turned into introducing my son Kevin to his son Tom, and today

Kevin is the host of the widely popular podcast *The Ziglar Show*, now with more than 41 million downloads. Mark Victor Hansen invited me to come share how attendance at his Mega Book Marketing University opened the door for my first book deal with *48 Days to the Work (and Life) You Love* and how that led to a bidding war for my second book. The ripple effect of those connections led to the opportunity to create a six-hour audio program with Nightingale-Conant titled "Dream Job." And that put me into that illustrious category of what I had always referred to as the Masters of Achievement. Today that audio program is ranked third in customer response, right above the number four program, "The Strangest Secret," by Earl Nightingale himself.

Several months after selling that fitness center and realizing I was deeply in debt, I met a guy named Dave Ramsey at the church we both attended. Dave had recently crashed financially as well. We became friends and brainstormed about the businesses we wanted to build. He wanted to help people avoid the financial mistakes he had made, and I wanted to help people apply their strongest passions in work that was meaningful, purposeful, and profitable. Soon thereafter, Dave had the opportunity to get on the radio in Nashville. He quickly gained a following with his common sense principles. But many of his listeners clearly needed to make more income, and he would send them to me, his trusted friend, to get the resources they needed. Today Dave has over 14 million listeners weekly—and he still refers them to me daily.

Dr. Glenn Vo is a master connector. He understands the power of those personal connections. But now he combines that power with the technology tools that allow this expanded influence to be put in place in far less time than what was possible 20 years ago. Absorb this book, apply the practices presented, and become your own *Industry Influencer*.

—Dan Miller, *New York Times* best-selling author, *48 Days to the Work (and Life) You Love*, 48Days.com

Preface

As he stared out at the pond, the painful memory of the accident returned ... the headlights growing brighter and brighter. The horn blaring. The deafening sound of metal crunching as the car wrapped around the oak tree at 2612 Cherryhill Lane. He felt guilty about it every day and had learned to stifle the memory into the depths of his mind. He tried not to think about Gabby but he remembered her sweet, smiling face every time he looked down at his amputated legs. They were a constant reminder that he ruined his football career, took his little sister's life, and destroyed his relationship with his dad, all because he couldn't refrain from texting Lacey back after she sent him that picture.

This is an excerpt from a novel called *2612 Cherryhill Lane* I recently wrote. Not unusual. Plenty of people from all professions publish books every year.

What *is* unusual is the way social media has marketed my novel.

Thousands of people "liked" *2612 Cherryhill Lane* on Facebook long before it was published. Without typing up a press release, reaching out to book reviewers, or scheduling speaking engagements, I plugged into the power of online influence to generate more anticipation than I ever imagined. Even before I released the book, I had 12,000 followers.

And that's what *this* book is all about—growing your brand by using meaningful connections in social engagement. In other words, becoming an industry influencer, and the type of industry influencer that goes beyond Instagram posts of #fashion and YouTube spins on "Baby Shark."

Do you have something important to say?

Do you have something important to share with your industry?

Do you want to impact more people than just those within the four walls of your office or practice?

If the answers are yes, you already have the drive to become an industry influencer.

For professionals, industry influence is the ability to bring our expertise to the 3.5 billion people now on social media in the best, most neatly packaged way possible.

Think about how you might become an influencer off-line, for a moment. Let's say you were bringing a box of your finest financial advice to the Queen of England. You wouldn't wrap it in newspaper or duct tape, right? You would order some pretty fancy wrapping paper and ribbon, crease the edges just right, and attach a hand-written note on letterpress—or at least have someone else do it for you. You would carefully choose how you package and position your advice before sending it to the Queen, wouldn't you? Yet way too many people just jump online without thinking and wonder why nobody is paying attention to them. In many cases, it's because they didn't apply the time-tested methods of influence to the online world. Becoming an industry influencer in an online world follows the same principles as the off-line world. We just need to apply those principles to the virtual world. Like with the off-line world, it starts with picking a niche. From there, we strategize what your digital footprint will look like. Then, we establish, polish, and expand your online presence. There is no end to the possibilities of your influence when you take this approach.

> "Start right now," says Vidya Ravi, CEO of Storybird Ads, of building a niche influence. "Just start and you will figure out a way if your intentions are right and strong."

Even better, with this approach, you don't have to quit your day job to do it well. I should know: I'm a full-time practicing dentist with a thriving practice in Texas. I still have my day job, yet in 2017 I created another business, NiftyThriftyDentists.com, a website and podcast that has influenced dental professionals all over the world with money-saving tips, strategies, and resources. I've also turned around and done something *completely* different by writing and promoting a work of fiction. That story sat inside me for years. Now, I get to hold it in my hands and celebrate the success it achieved hitting the *USA Today* best-seller's list. How I wrote and promoted *2612 Cher-*

ryhill Lane is also a case study to show you that what I'm about to reveal in *this* book works. I used the same methods I share with you to build Nifty Thrifty Dentists as well as to promote *2612 Cherryhill Lane*. And I've helped many other people establish and grow their influence using these methods too.

The best part about the system is how simple it is. That's part of the reason it works so well: anyone can use it to build their reputation in *any* niche. And that's why I wrote this book. I wrote this book *not* to prove a point or add another book to my bookshelf. But I wanted to help other people break out of the mundane, expand beyond their day jobs, and build a part- or full-time business helping to shape the industry of their choosing. Follow these steps and you, too, can make an impact. You can improve an industry for generations to come.

Let's turn back to NiftyThriftyDentists.com for a moment. When I decided to do something significant beyond the four walls of my practice, I chose to work with a strategic coach. I had seen others build businesses on the side and wanted to benefit from what they had learned before me. In doing so, I discovered my own unique passion and ability as a connector. I love connecting with other people as well as helping to connect people with others. I also love helping businesses grow and helping business owners save money.

Those talents and passions became the core of Nifty Thrifty Dentists, which has offered win-win scenarios to vendors and dentists by negotiating discounts for dental professionals. NiftyThriftyDentists.com has helped me connect dental professionals with the discounts I've negotiated.

The vendors have appreciated the opportunity to be featured in front of thousands of dentists and have paid me a commission every time someone in my community has purchased from them. The dentists in my community have appreciated both the discount and the fact that I've vetted each vendor before recommending them. By earning the commission, Nifty Thrifty Dentists' business model has become a true triple win. My community has saved money. The companies have reached more people. And I've earned money by finding high-quality products and services and negotiating deals for my community.

This is how I first impacted and influenced my industry while still keeping my day job. But it's just one way to become an industry influencer. And that's the beautiful part of becoming an industry influencer. You get to choose your own adventure. No matter what path you choose, however, the steps to achieving your goal remain the same. For the rest of this book, I'll walk you through those steps.

Whether you're marketing a GPS-enabled umbrella business, hoping to sell $2 million more in bubble tea, or simply wanting to rise to the top of "car dealerships near me" searches, *Industry Influencer* can help you achieve your goal.

By the last page (perhaps even by now), you'll become excited and empowered to tap into the best-kept secret in business—the power of you! And you'll learn that you can truly build influence in your industry while eating a bowl of Cheerios, catching up on the latest Netflix series, or caring for dental patients all day, like me.

By doing so, you'll begin leading a more fulfilling, influential, and lucrative life—the life of an industry influencer.

Introduction

I f you're reading this book, you likely experienced at least part of the coronavirus or COVID-19 pandemic that swept the planet. Like Pearl Harbor, the assassination of John F. Kennedy, and the attacks of 9/11, the coronavirus pandemic is one of those history-making events with which you'll always remember exactly where you were and what you were doing as it happened. (Only, in this case, you were there for a *very long time*.)

And if you're reading this in the immediate aftermath of the pandemic, chances are you're one of millions trying to get back on your feet. As I began writing this book, I was wondering about the paychecks I needed to cut for my practice. But I was also part of a population that was doing everything it could to prepare for "normalcy" to return and see our work and our passions meet the needs of our industries. We were not making money, but we were spending time with our audiences through online platforms such as Facebook and Zoom.

We invested time, effort, and money to connect with the people with whom we built relationships through our brands. In my case, I spent time deepening relationships with people in the dental industry to help all dental professionals come out of the other side of the pandemic thriving. I also spent time with other industry influencers to help them continue to build their brands and support their own communities.

All this time and effort paid dividends throughout. It helped our communities navigate a tough time while showing them we care about them in good times and in bad. After all, in any industry, your brand is your professional reputation. What you do with—and through—your brand will determine your future. And when we look back at the pandemic, I'm sure we will see that the people who made the most consistent and meaningful connections with their communities throughout the pandemic were the ones who came out the strongest. That's because, with so much noise online, meaningful connections and engagement are more important than ever. People ache for meaning. They ache for true connections. If you provide that meaning, you will succeed. If not, you won't. It's that simple.

Many of us have shared our personal and professional strengths with others by establishing a presence online. Yet many people are still searching for momentum, or just how to bring their passions and expertise to their audience's attention.

Consider Dr. Anissa Holmes. Anissa's a dentist. At one time, she was just an ordinary dentist fixing teeth and running a dental practice. She started practicing in 1999 and, for the first twelve years of her business, her practice was fairly routine. (If you're unfamiliar with the dental industry, "fairly routine" isn't really a good thing.)

Facing burnout, she found herself at a crossroads—burn out or go big. She decided to go big, hired a coach, invested in training, and implemented new strategies for her practice. She broke the mold of what the typical dentist was doing to market a practice, stopped traditional advertising altogether, and focused all her attention on Facebook marketing. As a result, her monthly new-patient numbers increased tenfold, from 15 to 150 with a marketing budget that was a fraction of what most practices spent. Her practice became extremely profitable, and she used those profits to build a new, state-of-the-art office, tripling her capacity. Her Facebook marketing techniques also attracted more than 50,000 fans to her practice's Facebook page while increasing her profits by 300%.

Having achieved that level of success for her practice, she could have sat back and enjoyed the profits. She could have hired a team to take over clinical care and not have to work. But she had a fire burning inside her to help other dentists achieve the same peace and profitability that she had. So she started sharing the strategies that had helped her practice grow.

In a few short years, Anissa became an extraordinary force among the millions of dentists practicing worldwide, all from her home in Jamaica, surrounded by palm trees and beaches. Anissa is able to influence people hundreds and thousands of miles away—all thanks to the magic of passion, perseverance, and social media.

Even better, she achieved all that influence without sacrificing her practice profits. She still gets dozens of new patients every month through Facebook with a budget of less than $500 per month. Meanwhile, dentists are forking over thousands of dollars a month to be part of her dental coaching program.

How does Anissa Holmes do it? She posts engaging content, she delivers engaging podcasts, and she wrote a book, *Delivering WOW*, that's become a blueprint for running and growing a successful dental practice. She not only created the content, she also maximized social engagement in her circles in order to become a dental influencer.

Anissa is one of my mentors—I've gone through her coaching program—but I share her story because it illustrates how simple it is to become an industry influencer if you take action.

We may not all oversee a worldwide business from the beaches of Jamaica someday, but if we follow the simple, proven plan to achieve industry influence, we can create our own versions of paradise while helping others improve their lives—just like Anissa did in the dental world.

Keep Your Day Job: Why It Works

One of the biggest challenges for people who want to become industry influencers is deciding what to do with their day jobs. Some people want to cling onto their day jobs as long as they can—sometimes to the point that it slows them down in their efforts to help people as industry influencers. Others want to quit today, believing that investing 100% of their time and focus to build their influence will help them achieve success faster.

So what's the right thing to do? Simple. Don't quit your day job—at least not yet. For now, hold on. As we build, you'll get a better understanding of when it will be smart to take the leap, if ever. In fact, you might never quit your day job. Anissa still runs her practice. You don't have to ever quit your day job to build an impactful and lucrative business as an industry influencer. If and when you quit is a decision for another day when you have better information available than you do right now.

It can seem overwhelming to suddenly become an industry influencer, especially with a day job, family, and other obligations. But if you've picked up this book, I bet you already know that *somehow* you can make a bigger impact, whether it's on your profession, your bank account, your family, your community, or the world. You just need to know *how*.

While you might not believe it yet, I know you can become an industry influencer because you—like everyone I have ever met—have what I refer to as a Triangle of Genius, which is the key to making a successful transition to becoming a successful industry influencer. We'll discuss the concept throughout this book. For now, just know that you have it. I'll teach you how to find it—and what to do with this Triangle of Genius to increase your industry influence later in the book. So don't consider quitting your day job at least until you understand your Triangle of Genius and start using it profitably as an industry influencer. This isn't the moment to reenact a movie scene where you suddenly storm into your boss's office and, to the soundtrack of some '80s movie, declare, "I quit!" (Unless you really want it to be and have the ability to take care of all your needs without any income for a while. If that's you, great. But if it's not you, don't quit your day job today.) The Triangle of Genius simply doesn't pull you away from your day job. Quitting your day job needs to be an intentional, calculated decision.

But this *is* the moment to start building your industry influence so you can gather the data and experience to make a better decision about your future. Take advantage of just a few fast and free resources to grow your business, connect with thousands—if not millions—of people and find some pretty amazing growth in yourself too. All of these resources are right at your fingertips, or at least around the corner at the local library. Without pulling all-nighters, draining our savings account, or leaving my full-time dental practice, I was able to discover incredible influence, and you can too.

"It is absolutely possible to build industry influence while working full-time," says Laine Schmidt, a Florida-based business coach. "Planning and use of tools is the best way to optimize limited time. Plan a month of your social media posts and then put them into a tool such as Buffer, Hootsuite, or any other social media manager, and take a step back to let the magic happen. Your job after that will be to respond to comments and measure which posts are most helpful for your audience based on engagement you're getting. The more frequent your posts, the more consistent your growth will be."

New Opportunities Appear Frequently with Social Media

Clubhouse is one of the latest social media platforms for sharing, collaborating, and discussing using voice-only technology. On Clubhouse, you're able to join any chat room about anything. This app can be used for seminars, networking, collaborations, podcast communities, and the list goes on. The person who starts a chat room gets to be the moderator and can appoint other people to talk whenever someone has something to add to the conversation. When you join a chat, you join as a listener and cannot unmute yourself unless a moderator gives you permission. With Clubhouse, you can broaden your networks vastly. It offers the opportunity to connect with other professionals from different industries than your own.

The numbers speak for themselves.

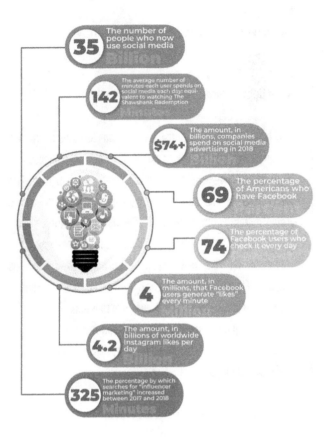

At age 19, Jason Wong made $200,000 in just three weeks on social media when he released parts of *The Holy Méme Bible*—and that was just the beginning for him. Wong also took to Twitter, inventing a profile to promote his book, which was ultimately published by traditional media. His projected forecasted earnings from *The Holy Méme Bible* and its promotional products hovered around $1 million, all from scrolling through social media.

On Instagram alone, influencer marketing is now a $2 billion-plus industry, with Kylie Jenner perhaps the most famous example of cashing in on the trend. (Think $1.2 million per Instagram post.) The Rock, Beyoncé, and Selena Gomez help round out the top-10 money-making list, but if you're working for the same reasons I am—to make an impact—forget about celebrity status and start focusing on what might be in your wheelhouse and you can still make great money as an influencer. For example, "nursefluencers" fill Instagram feeds all around the world, beekeepers have built massive TikTok audiences, and one Seattle nonprofit crusader has amassed more than 16,000 followers on Twitter. If you have a passion, you can build an audience.

Facebook "Lives," or live video broadcasts on Facebook, meanwhile, have made it even easier to increase our online presence. In 2018, the number of Facebook Live broadcasts reached 3.5 billion, covering everything from Kohl's shoppers and Tough Mudder training to mascara application and "man on the street" interviews. Facebook Live is a regular feature on Nifty Thrifty Dentists, and I've also used the video feature to share *2612 Cherryhill Lane*.

Finally, even if your day job gobbles up too much of your time, you can shortcut your path to success in many ways. Use this book as a workbook and follow step-by-step during breaks or after the kids go to bed, for example. Or, if you want even more depth and help, you can invest in a course, such as my Side Gig Multiplier program, which you can check out at drglennvo.com/resources, which includes a collection of courses to help you build and grow a side gig. Well-designed courses can help you cut down the learning curve even more to find the best use of whatever limited time you have.

You definitely don't have to go it alone.

We're Wired This Way: How It Works

The studies of social media influence are new, but the science behind industry influence dates back to the dawn of humankind when we sat around the fire not only to stay warm but also to connect with our fellow human beings. Those humans could warn us of an approaching woolly mammoth or share a new tool they created: these simple lessons helped propagate the species.

For all the grumpy cat memes and money-making schemes on the Internet, research shows some surprisingly good news about industry influence. For example, research from the *New York Times* and Foundation Marketing discovered five main reasons we share content online:[1]

1. To improve the lives of others: A whopping 94% of people said they share because they believe that the content will improve the lives of their audience.

---

1   Team, Foundation. "The Psychology Of Content Sharing Online In 2021 [Research]." *Foundation Marketing*, 10 Feb. 2021, foundationinc.co/lab/psychology-sharing-content-online/.

2. To define themselves: Most of us want to look better, right? Well, at least 68% of us, who share content to create an "idealized online persona."
3. To stay connected with others.
4. Self-fulfillment.
5. To publicize the causes they care about: The study found that 84% of participants say they share information "as a way to support causes or brands they care about."

Meanwhile, 65% of us are visual learners—naturally inclined to find answers in compelling videos and posts on Facebook, Instagram, and other top social media channels. We also release natural feel-good endorphins when we connect with and feel accepted by others. And numerous studies have shown that we're more likely to share positive content. Storytelling touches something primal in us, and when we share good news, we're more likely to set off a cascading effect.

But enough with the numbers. Let's get started on the simple steps to making an impact through industry influence. Throughout this book, I'll share straightforward stories that illustrate why and how industry influence can work with you, punctuated by friendly instructions on what to do next.

You'll also see that each chapter concludes with a "Creating Your Triangle of Genius" section giving you the easy essentials to do it right.

I've also created an online platform of resources, courses, and other tools to help you go from ordinary to extraordinary in less time than it takes to get your teeth cleaned.

Chapter 1:

Picking a Niche

———

My wife and I *love* saving money. As co-owners of a dental practice, we kind of have to love saving money. It costs around $500,000 to start a practice today; add another $250,000 or so for remodeling, plus $200,000 for equipment and $70,000 for marketing—not to mention employee salaries and other expenses.

With all that spending, we've spent years looking for deals and bargains to grow our business, combing through the Dental Garage Sale Facebook group and creating dealer relationships for ongoing discounts.

For years, our passion for finding discounts created excitement on a small scale. Little did I know that this passion and talent for saving money would become the first niche I'd choose to feed my desire to become a dental industry influencer.

So, what is a "niche," anyway? If you've thought about becoming an industry influencer before, you've likely heard the term already. If not, don't worry. I'll walk you through exactly what you need to know about the term over the rest of this chapter. Way too many people overcomplicate it when they teach it. Keep it simple and you'll be much better off in the long run. I'll help you do exactly that.

> "Think about what it is that you love doing, so much, that you would do it even for free," says Gonzalo Jimenez, funnel strategist for We Build Funnels. "What is it that comes so natural to you, that it doesn't even seem like work? If something seems too easy for you but too hard for others, that may be a good niche to explore."

What Are You Good At? What Gives You Passion?

As I mentioned in the introduction, I went through the coaching program offered by Anissa Holmes in 2017 to help grow my practice. At the end of the program, I was feeling pretty good about the tactics I was bringing back to my practice: chiefly creating a culture that celebrated the goals and dreams of each team member. I was tapping into the Dale Carnegie school of thought, discovering how to show my interest in other people and buying into what my team ultimately wanted.

Then Anissa said something that changed my life. She said, "Hey Glenn, what's next?"

What's next?! I thought to myself. *What does she mean, what's next?*

"Um, what do you mean, what's next?" I asked.

"What's next?" she repeated. "Because I see in you the ability to impact more people than just through your practice."

I had always dreamed of becoming an influencer, but Anissa's question still surprised me. The fact that she saw in me the ability to do so also got me excited.

I hadn't yet thought about how I wanted to influence people beyond my practice, so Anissa shared with me the power of creating engaging content. By doing so, she thought it would help me visualize what it might be like to become an influencer and help me find a niche that I enjoyed enough to create consistent content.

Anissa taught me that creating engaging content goes far beyond the surface level that most people focus on. That surface level is Level 1 content creation. Think of how you typically meet someone at a business function or meeting. You exchange cards with your website(s) listed on the card. They go to your site and see that you've published a few articles or videos. No matter how detailed it is, it's limited to what's on your site. What do they do next? Many people will google you next. By googling you, they go beyond Level 1 and see *all this content* you've produced along with everything that's been said about you online. You've gone from one-dimensional to three-dimensional in a nanosecond—you don't control everything they see on a Google search like you do on your website. And three-dimensional is a lot more compelling, interesting, and revealing.

That got me thinking about what I could do for the dental industry. If someone googled me, they'd have found my website, a bunch of dental review sites, and that's pretty much it. That's pretty boring. I wanted my Google search results to be much more interesting than that. I wanted to do something I was both passionate about and good at—something that would not only make it easy for me to create content but also give me the opportunity to have a positive, long-lasting effect on people.

I left that discussion without knowing exactly *what* I would do. But I knew I would do *something* that would make Google search results much more interesting.

What are you going to be—a coach? I asked myself. *What do you coach on? Do you coach on overhead management?*

Yes! I thought. *I do that for dentists, and I also provide marketing and leadership tips …*

I initially thought about my niche as just "helping dentists" and my audience focus as the "dental industry." But I quickly realized my actual niche is much narrower than that. Yes, I loved helping dentists. Yes, I loved saving money. But what I *really* loved was connecting people—but connecting in ways that created mutually beneficial relationships. I was always really good at getting discounts. And I knew I could galvanize a group of people to get discounts. The wheels started spinning.

Quickly thereafter, Nifty Thrifty Dentists was born, growing out of the Dental Garage Sale Facebook group I had run for a while, eventually taking on its own life. Today, Nifty Thrifty Dentists includes a website offering dental discounts, a blog, and a podcast with nearly 1 million downloads to date. Nifty Thrifty Dentists has grown in influence and has galvanized an industry to give back to the community through one of my favorite events, the Spirit of Giving Event, which involves dental vendors and coaches giving back to dentists who are struggling and in need.

> "It's always best to niche down as much as possible so that you'll actually stand out," says Wendy Conklin, chair stylist, designer, and teacher at Chair Whimsy. "The biggest mistake is trying to be like everyone else. Be different, and be bold about it. Then, success comes by serving your audience and listening to what they are asking you for. When they ask, deliver it to them. Stop doing what you want and do what they need. It's that simple."

Even better, we now have more than 30,000 members in the Facebook group for Nifty Thrifty Dentists, where anybody in the world can ask anybody else in the world such questions as

"What options do we have for an answering service?"

"Where can I get the most affordable supplies?"

and

"Do y'all use anything to send patient satisfaction surveys?"

Our Facebook Live videos, along with videos submitted by fans and followers, have created a dynamic forum where dental professionals can find around-the-clock discounts, advice, support, and more.

> "Build the narrowest niche possible and you will become the only choice in that market," says Colleen Kochannek, founder of the Scrappy Frontier, who started her first online business in 2017, after getting laid off from a 25-plus year corporate career. She now helps women from the "typewriter generation" become successful laptop entrepreneurs. "Your ability to impact that niche will be tremendous."

Remember, anyone can have this kind of influence. A recent study by the Digital Marketing Institute found that 49% of consumers depend on influencers for decision-making about online purchases.[2] This benefits the companies making the products, but it can benefit you too.

Dialing for Dollars

Once I determined my niche, it was time to get to work. I knew my niche would be helping people save money in the dental business and connecting them with the companies that were willing to work with them. From there, I needed to start creating content to get noticed in that niche.

---

2   Digital Marketing Institute, "20 Influencer Marketing Statistics That Will Surprise You," Digital Marketing Institute (Digital Marketing Institute, October 25, 2018), https://digitalmarketinginstitute.com/blog/20-influencer-marketing-statistics-that-will-surprise-you.

Because I was passionate about creating those triple-win scenarios, I was able to create real, valuable content pretty easily. It was, and is, a win-win-win—because I also make money—to negotiate deals and present them to dental professionals. (In basic terms, what I do is called affiliate marketing: making money recommending other people's products in exchange for a commission. Affiliate marketing is one of the quickest ways to monetize a niche because you don't need to create anything. You just need to find quality products, from a quality company, and promote them to an audience that trusts your recommendations. I was good at it too. My passion and natural talent for finding deals and making connections not only made affiliate marketing a natural fit, it made it enjoyable too.)

One of the best parts about affiliate marketing is how easy it is to get started, especially in an industry you know well. Many companies have formal affiliate programs you can sign up for right on their sites. The ones that don't are often open to deals once you have built a bit of an audience. So why not make money doing something you can do well, like affiliate marketing? That's actually what's going to keep you interested. You can find affiliate opportunities in any niche too. As long as there are products and services already being offered to your audience, you can find products to promote.

Let's say you're a personal trainer. And what you're *really* interested in is powerlifting. You've taught cardio classes and you've taught Spin classes; you've even jumped in the water with your Reeboks to teach water aerobics.

But all that has left you feeling flat. Instead, you *love* lifting heavy weight, and you *love* helping other people lift heavy weight. So maybe it's time to step away from the Spin class and focus on your niche—not only in the gym but also at home, where you can post money-making content. I can personally vouch for the motivation. Dinner is done, the kids are in bed, and you have a choice between collapsing on the couch for another Netflix episode or posting new content about powerlifting. If you know some money is going to come your way from the powerlifting post—which is also going to help others interested in powerlifting—I'll bet you'll choose that route.

> "A micro-influencer, which is someone that has 10,000 to 50,000 followers, is actually pretty valuable. They used to only pick up a couple hundred bucks, but today, they get a minimum of a few thousand dollars a post. Influencers with up to 1 million followers can get $10,000 [per post], depending on the platform, and 1 million followers and up, you're getting into territory where they can charge $100,000. Some can even get $250,000 for a post!"
> —**Joe Gagliese**, cofounder of Viral Nation

And with the advice in this book along with a little bit of luck, you may be one of the first to claim your niche, which is huge. It makes you the authority, just as I became with Nifty Thrifty Dentists. I was the first to negotiate the deals and discounts and the first to create the group. Now, there are other groups out there doing the same thing as Nifty Thrifty Dentists. Since then, others have attempted to do similar things in the dental industry. You'll find copycats, too, especially as you become more known. But when people copy you, they actually validate you. You're doing something right if they want to copy you. But when you find something you're passionate about, you will almost always be a few steps ahead of the copycats, especially if the copycats choose to enter your niche because they see you making money and not because it's a true passion of theirs. When you match your niche to a true passion, like I did with Nifty Thrifty Dentists, you will almost always outwork the others because you will enjoy the work while they will see the work as a chore.

Your Triangle of Genius

Here's my No. 1 way to identify your niche and increase your industry influence: Your Triangle of Genius. It's loosely based on *The Legend of Zelda*, an action-adventure video game—one of Nintendo's most popular franchises. In the game you play as Link, a heroic elf who is given the monumental task of retrieving the mythical Triforce.

In *The Legend of Zelda*, the Triforce is made up of three components: the Triforce of Power, the Triforce of Wisdom, and the Triforce of Courage. When the Triforce is fully assembled, the owner is granted as many wishes as they want until they lose the Triforce. The goal of the game is to get the fully assembled Triforce before the evil Ganon does and to save the Princess in the process.

"Build your niche around something you enjoy; something that still piques your curiosity," says Jeane Sumner, founder of Website HQ. "The first part of that sounds a little cliché, but you will talk about it every day to everyone you meet and want to help. I also believe it should be something you have a natural curiosity about so that you want to keep learning and advancing your knowledge."

When figuring out your specific niche, you are also looking to assemble your very own Triforce—or what I like to call the Triangle of Genius. The Triangle of Genius includes three components that will lead you to your Genius Ability that you can use to make your wish of becoming an industry influencer come true.

The three components of your Triangle of Genius are Your Natural Talents, Your Passion, and Industry Needs. At the top of the Triangle is Your Natural Talents, and the two other components make up the base.

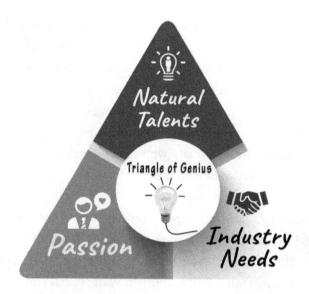

Simple, right? Almost too simple? That's important. Simple works. Let's break down each component:

1. **Your Natural Talents:** This is what you are good at. Everyone likes to be good at something, and it's best to work off of Your Natural Talents. My strengths are my ability to connect with people and to create "win-win" relationships. I was able to use these strengths to create a profitable affiliate marketing business in dentistry.

2. **Your Passions:** When you love something *and* you are good at it, then it's not really "work," right? It also means that you will be extremely motivated and determined to succeed. I am passionate about creating meaningful relationships. I am also passionate about dentistry. I created a platform to help

my fellow dentists while also creating meaningful relationships with many of my group members.

3. **Industry Needs:** Your industry must actually need your help before you provide it. I saw a need for dental professionals to save money. So I created a platform to help negotiate discounts and deals for dental professionals who can now decrease their overhead and save money.

You must have all three components of the Triangle of Genius to unlock your Genius Ability and make your wish of becoming an industry influencer come true. That's because your Genius Ability is your special ability to impact your community that nobody else has. Only you have it. Your community members will be able to *feel* it too. (They'll be able to feel that the copycats lack it as well.)

> "Start with the why," says Tamara Zantell, founder and CEO of Raising a Mogul. "Take the time to get clear on the purpose you want to serve, the humans you want to serve, and how your brand or business will solve their problems. Consider all the ways you can help them operate on a higher, more purposeful, powerful level simply by operating in your zone of genius with ease."

From NFL to Personal Growth

If you watched NFL football in the late '90s and early 2000s, you might know a guy named Alex Molden. Alex played in the NFL as defensive back for the New Orleans Saints, the San Diego Chargers, and the Detroit Lions between 1996 and 2004 before finding himself at a crossroads. After retiring, he needed to pivot to a new career. He wanted to build a personal brand. But he struggled to identify what his brand would be. "Your brand is really like your character," says Alex. "My brand should represent who I am. The biggest thing I had going for me was playing football. So when I stepped away, I was lost. Football was no longer my brand, like it had been for so many years, so I felt like I was walking around lost. My identity had been wrapped up in football because I'd been playing for so long—since I was 11 or 12 years old."

Alex thought about how he could be more impactful and what really gave him passion after playing football. "I love helping people, so I thought, 'OK, how do I help people?'" he recalls today. "Well, I could help them reach their athletic potential. After all, after I retired from the NFL, I had been working with people who wanted to become better athletes. And I loved doing so. Thus, I started looking to build relationships to continue to grow my reputation in the athletic training world."

Once Alex became clear about his strengths, passions, and industry needs, it became much easier for him to build his influence. He started by reaching out to his former coaches, who pointed him to the right certifications and seminars that would help him add to his résumé while meeting other people in the fitness world. While he didn't think of it this way at the time, Alex had discovered his Triangle of Genius, and that made it much easier for him to grow his influence.

He also closely watched people in the industry he admired, studying their cues of how to talk to athletes and what they did to help. Today, Alex is a leadership and development speaker and coach, as well as the host of the popular *The Shark Effect* podcast, which examines the qualities of high performers and how they lead.

"You can influence people through leadership, but it all boils down to people," says Alex. Think of it as a framework around your Triangle of Genius: all of the people you influence, and how they influence you in return.

From Dental Hygiene to Dental Education Cruises

But what if you're not a retired NFL player, like Alex Molden? Can you still make it happen? Of course you can. I did from the safety of my dental office. Elijah Desmond did too. Elijah graduated from The Ohio State University with a degree in dental hygiene. He soon discovered, though, that while he was good at dental hygiene, he wasn't as passionate about being a dental hygienist as he was about starting businesses and motivational speaking—we're talking super energetic motivational speaking, in super fun settings.

The deeper Elijah got into the dental world, the more of a need he saw for rejuvenating continuing education programming to make it both informative *and* fun. That led to Elijah starting a company called Smiles at Sea, which takes groups of dental professionals on cruise ships to learn, vacation, *and* party.

"I wanted to start something super unique with vacation and education on a cruise," says Elijah. "I thought, *Why not bring the top educators from around the world and put them on a ship?*" In its first year, Smiles at Sea drew 269 dental professionals; today Royal Caribbean's entire *Oasis of the Sea* ship fills up with thousands of dental professionals for a four-day sail between Miami and Nassau. "It's a professional environment, but it allows people to let down their hair and actually be themselves," says Elijah. "And there's literally entertainment from when you wake up until it's time to go to bed. We're like a dental festival." Elijah continues to innovate with Smiles at Sea, too, adding speaking competitions to help new speakers break in, creating land-only events, and more.

Elijah makes money sipping strawberry daiquiris underneath the palm trees, and it's all part of making money while helping people through his Triangle of Genius. (Many might even argue that this is the pinnacle of the Triangle of Genius.)

Your Why and Your Ikigai

In some ways, the Triangle of Genius also represents our sense of purpose, or our "why" in life—what drives us to immediately turn off the alarm clock and hop out of bed to start the day instead of hitting snooze. In Japan, this concept is called *ikigai* (pronounced "ee-key-guy") and roughly translates to "the happiness of always being busy," and it's been explained as one reason why people in Japan live so long. For every 100,000 people on the island of Okinawa, there's an average of 24.55 people over the age of 100, which is way more than the average around the world.

Here's a diagram of *ikigai* that Héctor García and Francesc Miralles share in *Ikigai: The Japanese Secret to a Long and Happy Life*:

As García and Miralles write: "Nurturing friendships, eating light, getting enough rest, and doing regular, moderate exercise are all part of the equation of good health, but at the heart of the joie de vivre that inspires these centenarians to keep celebrating their birthdays and cherishing each new day is their *ikigai*."

Why Willpower Doesn't Work

In some ways, *ikigai* explains the premise behind *Willpower Doesn't Work*, a great book by Benjamin Hardy about how our environment shapes our successes (or failures). White-knuckling our way through tough situations, he writes, is a fad, a fallacy—something that leads to little more than, well, white knuckles.

So what do we do instead? Well, we need to create and control our own situations instead of using grit to get through our current cultural addictions. And we can do so much easier when our work falls straight in our *ikigai*.

Technology is moving so fast, we can barely adapt. We're under constant stress and sleep deprivation, putting us in survival mode. As Hardy writes: "Most people are casualties of these rapid environmental changes. Unequipped to properly govern themselves in a new world with new rules, many of them succumb to various addictions—primarily to technology, but also to stimulants such as caffeine, fast-absorbing foods containing high amounts of carbohydrates and sugar, and work."

Hey, I've definitely succumbed to these things, but I never really thought of them as *addictions*. Addictions are alcohol, drugs, gambling, right? Nope, it can be anything that gets us to keep pushing that trigger to get us through the day in some zombie-like way. Technology can be a good thing—we're all using it right now, and it's created millions of marvels and saved millions of lives—but let's face it, if you're scrolling through Instagram posts of old girlfriends or googling how to melt butter instead of writing a blog post, you're addicted to technology and likely not working in your Triangle of Genius or *ikigai*.

> "Niche down," says Talia Browne of Rebel Love Media. "Find something that people are really passionate about that you're also passionate about, and go all in. Don't worry about fitting in a box or being like the others; really 100% being yourself seems to connect more than you think."

When I have the temptation to scroll aimlessly through social media, I put in an action that counteracts it. I plan ahead, too, preparing myself mentally to take a positive action, like doing some push-ups or drinking a glass of water when I catch myself. That works very well in the short term. But the long-term approach I've started using, thanks to *Willpower Doesn't Work*, is to spend time each day focusing on my "why" power. To step back for a moment, every day, to focus on my "why." This rewires my brain to focus in the right direction from the start.

When you think about using willpower to stop negative behavior, our internal dialog goes along the lines of, "Hey, I'm not supposed to eat that chocolate chip cookie because I'm trying to lose weight." So you use your willpower to tell yourself, "I'm just going to resist it." Over time, however, that willpower isn't strong enough. Our minds and bodies become desensitized to that script.

Developing a "why" power and spending time each day proactively focusing on our why hits a bit deeper. You go into the day prepared to skip the cookie. Maybe your family has a history of heart disease and you want to be healthy, avoid certain medications, and be there for your kids long into their adulthood. Or maybe you want to lose weight because you want to look great for a speaking engagement. Just a few minutes of focus every day helps avoid temptation much better than trying to catch yourself in the moment.

This can apply to any situation. I love Dr Pepper, for example. But I don't drink it—or maybe once or twice a year at most—because I know that sugar will lead to tooth decay. As a dentist, I can't be a hypocrite. I want to inspire my patients to live a healthier life. That's a big part of who I am as a dentist. That's my "why" power. So, instead of trying to catch myself in the moment, I avoid Dr Pepper and many other temptations by reminding myself of my "why" power as a dentist.

This can apply to almost any situation: binge-watching Netflix, being on autopilot for another trip to the Starbucks drive-through, purposely scheduling back-to-back meetings that keep you from getting your work done so you can go home to your family.

So when it comes to the discipline of doing the work to build and maintain industry influence, take some time to channel your "why" power and you will help avoid many of the common distractions that keep people from building consistent momentum.

Gut Check

Before you go any further, do a gut check. Do you have an idea of what your niche might be? Ask yourself whether it checks all three boxes. Are you passionate about the topic? Do you have a base level of relevant talent you can build upon? And does your niche match a need that people in a well-defined group are looking for? If so, you are setting yourself up for success. If not, how can you shift your focus slightly to check all three boxes?

For example, I have been a server in two different professions—as a dentist and also as a waiter for two well-known restaurants. The first restaurant was a fondue place that eventually folded into the Melting Pot franchise. A meal lasts a little bit longer at The Melting Pot, where many people celebrate special occasions or simply indulge in cheese and chocolate. For waiters who work on tips, people sitting for a while is bad for business—unless they keep adding to their tab. So my strategy was to upsell to higher-priced entrées and keep selling as they sat and talked. I could get customers to order the lobster tails or an extra salad, or add Grand Marnier to their chocolate fondue. After all, a bigger bill meant a bigger tip. The second restaurant was TGI Fridays—a very fast-paced restaurant that made money by turning tables as fast as possible. That was our customers' focus too. Hardly anybody went to TGI Fridays to spend hours celebrating special events. They went for a quality meal and fun atmosphere but not for a three-hour dinner. So, while working there, I focused mostly on turning tables as quickly as I could.

I was good at waiting tables, and the industry always needs good servers. I'll probably nudge my own kids to wait tables someday. If nothing else, it creates more respect for people in the service industry. But it also helps build a customer service muscle you can't get anywhere else.

While I did well in the restaurant industry, I wasn't passionate about the restaurant business. Thus, the restaurant industry only checked two boxes: strength and need. My lack of passion made the restaurant world a poor fit for industry influence in the long run. I like to eat, and that's about all I want to do in a restaurant these days.

Just because we're good at something doesn't mean we're passionate about it. But when you can combine those three factors and get into that niche, you create an unstoppable force.

So, before moving forward, give yourself a gut check about your niche to make sure it checks all three boxes.

Carving Out a New Niche

So what do you do if you realize your niche doesn't check all three boxes? Simple. You choose a new one. That's the great thing about niches. You can change direction at any time. And there's no better time to change your niche than the moment you realize it doesn't fit your Triangle of Genius. In fact, there's almost never a bad time to change direction, provided you know where you're going—and that you're still providing for your family.

For example, a friend of mine recently told me about some amazing charcuterie she'd discovered with a pretty neat niche story behind it. The charcutier grew up surrounded by fantastic food, as his mother managed a restaurant and his dad followed sophisticated and secret family recipes to cook elaborate meals.

But when this guy graduated from college, he went straight into the corporate world like many of his friends. He was miserable—and so enrolled in a culinary school, and then interned at the French Laundry where he found the fine art of charcuterie. He was good at selecting and slicing sausages and passionate about procuring pancetta and other meaty treats; and it turns out the country has a particular palate for pork, lamb, and duck products. Now, he's used his Triangle of Genius and industry influence to deliver the goods to gourmands in 48 states.

Another friend quit the practice of law after thirteen years to become a writer. Like me in the restaurant world, he was a great lawyer and made good money doing so, but he had no passion for the practice of law. So what did he do? He worked from 8:30 p.m. until his eyes closed searching for his passion. It took him a little while to find his Triangle of Genius while still practicing law 50–70 hours a week. But once he did, he was able to retire from the practice of law for good in his mid-thirties.

There's no better time than now to carve a new path for your life. In fact, although many negative things came out of COVID-19, one positive was how millions of Americans discovered or rediscovered old hobbies and hidden talents. One study found that 33% of Americans picked up arts and crafts during the coronavirus pandemic.[3] It may just be a temporary pastime, but it could serve as a launchpad for eventually sharing expertise and even making money from a creative outlet during COVID-19. Isolation can suddenly become engagement with thousands of followers and new friends. And even better, multiple studies have shown that the types of leisure activities that might emerge from sheltering in place as our Triangle of Genius can reduce stress and improve our overall mental and physical health.

From growing orchids and learning to play the piano to channeling lifelong skills toward a more lucrative pursuit and making career pivots, downtimes can turn up good things. Just look at the Facebook group "Asian Grub in DFDUB." Asian Grub in DFDUB was started on March 2020 by four friends who loved Asian food. Their goal in starting the group was simply to support area businesses that were forced to close their doors for indoor dining because of the pandemic.

In a matter of months, the group grew to more than 40,000 members (including me). All 40,000 members shared the founders' passion for Asian food and wanted to help businesses get through the pandemic. Together, we shared names of area Asian restaurants, bubble tea shops, dessert shops, and other Asian food stores we wanted to support. The members of the community then ordered

---

3   Amar Hussain, "Most Popular Hobbies during the Coronavirus Outbreak [Survey]," Nerd Bear, March 26, 2020, https://nerdbear.com/popular-hobbies-coronavirus-outbreak-survey/.

takeout food from those shops to support them during the lockdown. That community helped save dozens of local businesses, all by simply talking about local Asian restaurants in a Facebook group and ordering takeout food.

Asian Grub in DFDUB (DFW)
🔒 Private group · 41.6K members

About   Discussion   Announcements   Topics   Members   Events   Media   Files

Erin Wade Booke shared a link.
April 16 ·

Hi all! I'm the food editor at The Dallas Morning News, and our writer Amanda Albee has written a very informative piece on the boba situation. Thanks to all the tea shops who talked to us!

DALLASNEWS.COM
Boba shortage in Dallas: Smaller tea shops feeling the sting

Social media

Dallas-based Facebook group Asian Grub in DFDUB — with more than 38,000 members — has been especially helpful to Asian-owned restaurants during the pandemic. Started by five University of Texas at Arlington alumni, the group had 18,000 followers when *Dallas Observer*'s Brian Reinhart first reported its mission to save North Texas Asian restaurants.

In "The Science of Staying Connected," an April 2020 review published in the *Wall Street Journal,* psychologist Susan Pinker looks at our need to connect in a meaningful way.[4] "Evidence shows that social interaction is a biological requirement, much like eating, drinking and sleeping,"

---

4   Susan Pinker, "The Science of Staying Connected," *Wall Street Journal,* April 2, 2020, sec. Life, https://www.wsj.com/articles/the-science-of-staying-connected-11585835999.

writes Pinker. "Our ability to learn to talk, play, acquire new skills, fall in love, conduct business, and age in good health all hinge on our motivation to connect with other people." She brings up examples of how social media meets this primal need: a writer who posted a video of her husband using a welding torch to create crème brûlée and called it Fattening the Curve. Another post on Facebook shared a Bach suite from a cellist trying to soothe his friends and followers.

We definitely don't need a pandemic to discover our Triangles of Genius. But these stories prove that almost anything is possible—and that we can have a profound impact by sharing our niche with the world.

Start Ugly

So how do we get started? Here's some of the best advice I've ever heard, from podcasting guru and founder of Podfest Multimedia Expo, Chris Krimitsos: start ugly. In his book by the same name, *Start Ugly*, Krimitsos demonstrates how "starting ugly" was the foundation of how he became a major industry influencer. "Don't allow perfectionism, don't allow fear to strip you of starting," Krimitsos explains. "You need to start, make mistakes, and adjust as you learn more. All starts are ugly. But so many of us have this success or perfectionist mindset that holds us back from starting until we believe everything is perfect. Then, if something doesn't work right away, we count it as a failure and crawl back to a miserable day job or believe we can never succeed. I look at the ultimate failure as thinking about something and never doing anything about it. Start ugly, adjust as you go, and you can accomplish anything you want."

Creating Your Triangle of Genius

- Draw a triangle divided into three parts. In the top third, write Your Natural Talents. In the lower left third, write the needs of your industry—or perhaps another industry to which you could pivot. In the lower right third, write your passions. At the center is your Triangle of Genius.

- Before going any further, do a gut check, relying on your intuition to guide you toward the next step. Are you really ready to devote a significant amount of your time to your Triangle of Genius? Does it make you want to jump out of bed in the morning?

- Play *The Legend of Zelda* at zelda.com.

- Check out Alex Molden's story at alexmolden-speaks.com.

- Visit smilesatsea.com to learn more about how Elijah Desmond created a business in his Triangle of Genius. What can you learn from him?

- Be willing to start ugly.

- Consider reading these books:
  - » *The Seven Habits of Highly Effective People*, Stephen R. Covey
  - » *Ikigai: The Japanese Secret to a Long and Happy Life*, Héctor García and Francesc Miralles

- » *Willpower Doesn't Work*, Benjamin Hardy; benjaminhardy.com
- » *Start Ugly*, Chris Krimitsos; chriskrimitsos. com
- Visit drglennvo.com to discover tools, courses, books, and more.

Chapter 2:

Sharing Your Triangle of Genius

—

Ten years ago, author Chris Tuff thought his only expertise that mattered in the business world was the work he did for the Atlanta-based advertising agency 22Squared, where he worked helping companies make an impact through social media and other platforms.

In late 2016, however, he was near burnout and decided to take a month off from everything—his office, his family, even his iPhone—to reassess his life. When he emerged, he had changed many personal habits for the better and found his batteries recharged. One of the biggest changes he observed was how much better he empathized with many of his co-workers after his time away. In his case, he was put in charge of a new group of people, almost all of the millennial generation, and challenged to grow the group.

"Before taking time away, I was entirely focused on playing the rat race and trying to hit my metric of success without even thinking about what kind of impact I would make on the world," says Tuff. "But when I returned and was put in charge of a new group made entirely of people in the millennial generation, I quickly learned that we can be even more successful in ways that matter most when we focus just as much on the impact we make as we do on the success we achieve. For the first time ever, I saw myself as a cheerleader for a group of millennials. Their success became my success. Their fulfillment became my fulfillment. Their impact became my impact."

After shifting his focus to helping his team succeed, Tuff discovered a new passion for leadership that he never thought he had before. He also found a deep desire to share his new realization with the world to help other companies, leaders, and team members build similarly beneficial relationships.

What resulted was Tuff's first book, *The Millennial Whisperer*, a *USA Today* and *Los Angeles Times* best seller that has landed Chris lucrative speaking and consulting engagements around the world. Within one year of publishing the book, Chris landed engagements with companies like Nike, Cox Enterprises, LexisNexis, The Home Depot, and others, teaching executive teams how to build highly productive and motivated teams no matter what generation they belong to. He helps them lead with empathy and build positive, productive work cultures. His book has since been published in Portuguese and Spanish and led to a second book in the works called *Save Your Asks*, a new guide for networking your way into greater impact and success.

How's that for a Triangle of Genius? It's one that has completely turned Tuff's life around while helping others change their lives too. He used the powerful arenas of online and off-line networking to share his story of hitting a breaking point and discovering an expertise that can help companies and individuals. And he shared his story in such a way that it quickly positioned him as a highly sought-after leadership and culture expert.

> "Lead with tons of value, be genuine, be approachable, be welcoming, be compassionate, and maintain integrity in all things," says Julia Taylor, CEO and founder of GeekPack. "Continue to serve and empower your community beyond the sale. Build a community of raving fans."

Quickly Establishing Expertise without Having to Take a Month Away to Find Yourself

Like Chris Tuff, the fastest way to build your expertise is to start sharing your Triangle of Genius. While Chris did it by writing a book and engaging with people one-on-one, the easiest way to do it these days is to start sharing your story, your expertise, and your Triangle of Genius online. Start a blog. Share on social media. Hone your story and share it everywhere you can. Consistency is way more important than perfection when it comes to sharing your Triangle of Genius to build momentum as an industry influencer.

The great news is that "shareworthy" expertise can come from many sources—some of them accidental and surprising. With Tuff, for example, his education and professional background would never position him as a leadership expert. His passion and willingness to learn did. And, within one year, some of the biggest companies in the world were hiring him.

You don't have to dedicate your whole life to studying, say, Tai Chi, to become an expert or share your expert story. And you don't need to take a month off from everything to find yourself like Tuff did.

You can quickly make an impact just by taking action and doing things to position yourself as an expert, just like Tuff did. As an online industry influencer, you're pooling as many resources as possible to make an impact, and that can include linking to other experts and their sites. For example, one thing Tuff did to establish himself as a leadership expert was to lock arms with other experts and feature their strategies for leading millennials in his book.

If you practice Tai Chi, you can learn the principles and populate a website with some basic information that connects readers to others. Share your story and passion for Tai Chi, feature other experts, and continue to develop your expertise. This is all you need to do to create the beginning of your expert story.

In this "Golden Age of Expertise," I've found there are three ways you can become an expert:

- Expert by education
- Expert by experience
- Expert by passion

Expert by Education

I went to dental school, which is one element that goes into my becoming a dental expert. But I'm also continually educating myself to establish my niche within the dental industry. This is separate from my online industry influence. My "expert story" in dentistry is connecting the health of your teeth with the diet you consume. Each time patients come in, I go through their diet, and they are amazed because no other dentist talks about diet with their patients.

I explain that the food they're eating can have a big impact on their oral health. I warn them not to have an overly acidic diet, which can erode teeth. Acidic foods include coffee, alcohol, and processed foods. Some people are now proponents of an alkaline diet—full of fruits, vegetables, and legumes. I'm not here to give diet advice: this is just to share how continual education contributes to an ongoing expert story.

Now, as I write, hundreds of thousands of us have even more expertise by education, emerging from the COVID-19 crisis. Even if we haven't spent the spare time studying during the stay-at-home order, we've learned by simply listening to or reading the news about how to quarantine ourselves, how to shop for medical necessities, and how to cope with stress and anxiety. These skills are valuable not just for a one-time pandemic, but for any emergency that arises in the future. In 2017, the Centers for Disease Control and Prevention found that nearly 50% of Americans lacked even a basic emergency kit in their homes—COVID-19 changed that statistic for certain.

U.S. households, for example, took tips from the 5,000-member Reddit group called "PandemicPreps," whose members keep all the essentials on hand for emergencies. "A prepper is a person," one anonymous person told *Time* magazine, "who takes measures in advance to ensure the economic, physical and emotional well-being of their family during times of struggle."

We've learned even more from our online communities in the age of social distancing. We've seen Instagram posts on growing gardens. We've shared creative ideas on at-home graduations through Facebook. And we've learned how to turn isolation and loneliness into solidarity and solitude from LinkedIn—not to mention the millions of ideas from the millions of tweets filling our feeds.

My point here is to illustrate that education is everywhere, and opportunities can turn up at any time. Education goes beyond undergraduate degrees in finance, PhDs in psychology, or MDs in pediatrics.

Expert by Experience

Sometimes, you don't study to become an expert at something; you stumble into it instead. Chris Tuff didn't set out to become one of the world's top experts on corporate cultures and working with the millennial workforce; he went through a personal crisis and the school of hard knocks to discover his calling. History is rife with examples of experts who made mistake after mistake before making a name for themselves.

Thomas Edison famously said, "I have not failed 10,000 times—I have successfully found 10,000 ways that will not work." Benjamin Franklin was seriously electrocuted during one of his experiments. Oprah Winfrey's big-budget movie, *Beloved*, was a flop at the box office.

Electrocution, of course, is not exactly the best spark for industry influence. But failure is OK, and often even necessary to gain and share expertise. A recent University of Arizona study found that learning is optimized when we fail 15% of the time. One business coach based in Michigan shares the story of how he started a staffing company and, after incredible success, suddenly found himself $600,000 in debt and about to completely run out of cash in 60 days. He says this failure is the No. 1 reason he became a successful business coach. And recently, he's learned to pivot again by sharing the lessons he learned from failure in paid speaking engagements. It's the school of hard knocks, one that can be worth even more than an Ivy League degree or a PhD.

Or expertise can be just plain old *experience*. Let's say I wanted to write a book about being an effective waiter. Well, I didn't go to school to be a waiter, but I have more than 10 years of experience. I started as a busboy, clearing dishes, and worked my way up to the point where I was making some pretty good tips. So I have the expertise to share advice, make connections, and make an impact.

Expert by Passion

Never before has the world been so passionate about so much. Just look at YouTube, where more than 5 billion—yes, *billion*—videos are watched every day. These videos teach us everything from how to moonwalk or whistle with our fingers to saying the alphabet backward or beatboxing (or maybe both!), with some downright hilarious moments along the way. Of course, plenty of videos on YouTube and other platforms are serious, especially in the wake of COVID-19. But we're obviously hardwired to want to learn things. Studies show that learning is the No. 1 reason people want to join organizations—and most of us turn to our smartphones when we want to learn something.

We don't achieve mastery at first—it takes a long time to turn even our greatest passions into productivity and profit. It's like we're crash test dummies, absorbing the impact of a few missteps before discovering how to walk. I took the crash-test-dummy approach with my novel. I'd never written, let alone promoted, a novel before. But I was passionate about writing a novel, so I tested and experimented and figured it out, establishing a brand through social media. If nothing else, it shows a different side of me and how simply posting content can be a powerful tool. Posting content on Nifty Thrifty Dentists has allowed me to massively grow my dental brand within two years. This is something that has taken some people 10 years to do through old-fashioned networking.

Expert by Education, Experience, and Passion

Of course, there's a good chance your niche or Triangle of Genius stems from several sources, which reinforces your authenticity and authority.

A woman in my network, for example, has been taking a fitness class from the Les Mills franchise for more than 10 years and had often thought about what it would take to teach a session. When she was offered a chance to undergo free formal training to become an instructor, she knew the timing was right and spent a weekend learning how to perform the choreography and coach effectively from a certified trainer.

She also had more than 10 years of experience in taking the fitness class, which increased exponentially when she was part of the shelter-in-place of the COVID-19 pandemic, following the same routine day after day until she had all the moves memorized. Plus, she had incredible passion for a pastime that had helped her find physical and mental strength and a new network of friends.

Now, she not only gets paid for teaching part-time but is also setting up a social media presence that shares her education in, experience with, and passion for a health and wellness approach that can make an impact.

Establish Your Expertise: Connection and Engagement

As I've mentioned, my expertise has come from dental education, restaurant experience, and a passion for writing. But it can also come from your hobbies—cooking, playing the piano, rebuilding World War II planes, Zumba—the list is nearly endless, with many obvious and not-so-obvious opportunities.

Keep in mind that your expertise will grow as you build your platform for growing your brand. The key here is to also build genuine connection and engagement from the get-go, as it's the only way to leverage any kind of expertise you have and make an impact. If you want to become an authority figure, it's a good idea to attend conferences and summits, but today you have to go one step further in establishing a strong online presence.

Again, this may take some trial and error. For me on Facebook, for example, I've found certain posts more effective than others, and I've tested polls and videos. I started experimenting with these platforms for Nifty Thrifty Dentists and am essentially using the same concepts with my fiction book, which has about 13,000 followers.

Now, my expert story is showing readers how to grow a brand, not only through the pages of this book but also online. For me, any kind of meaningful connection and engagement is better than none. Even if only 30 dentists had joined Nifty Thrifty Dentists, I would have made an impact.

Why You Want to Build a Brand: Q&A with Amy Balog

Amy Balog is an executive coach and facilitator with ConnexionPoint Services in Atlanta. To add another perspective to this book and industry influence, in general, Amy took time to share about just why a brand is so important.

Glenn: So we have the big company brands—Nike, Apple, Whole Foods, Walgreens, but we also have our personal identity and then we have our job. But then we might have outside interests such as cooking, needlepoint, running, or driving race cars. So when we look into the future, and social media, because who knows what new version of LinkedIn or Facebook we might be on, why is it important to do some searching and establish that brand for yourself?

Amy: Well, people, your audience, are going to experience whatever it is that you're bringing to them. Think about anything that you participate in and have some loyalty to. How do you want to experience it yourself when you interact with either that product or that service person? And how do you imagine they will experience it themselves? It's like, OK, I can trust that every time I go back to that.

For example, I go to a remote workplace called Roam here in Atlanta. You can get a subscription for beautiful rooms and have gorgeous meetings. It's incredible. And every time I go to any location, I have this high-quality, beautiful experience. I feel like I'm in a warm, safe, attractive place. And I'm still paying my monthly subscription even though they're shut down by the coronavirus right now. Because I'm very loyal to that brand based on just how I feel and how my clients feel when we meet there. A brand is very tied to purpose. You don't know what you are if you don't have a purpose. Everything is purposeful. I'm going to help people get to a better place themselves. And I'm going to do it in specific ways.

Glenn: It really is all about purpose. So how do you engage your audience more, how do you get your name out there and start connecting? For example, someone who's learned to grow orchids in the midst of the coronavirus, and they become really good at it. And they want to, you know, increase their orchid business through social media. How do they start the right way?

Amy: Well, the beautiful thing about social media is that communities and groups share like interests. We were born to be connected. And it's not that hard to start establishing a place for yourself. Begin looking at where people or communities are gathering to discuss gardening, and then zone in on the orchids. You can build off your audience in a little bit of a dialog. Personally, I'm on LinkedIn a lot, and I don't do much on Twitter. Facebook some. But I don't do anything random. I try not to be thoughtless about any of it. So when I do make connections with people on social media, they're authentic.

Authority and Authenticity

As Amy's point on authenticity reminds us, the Golden Age of Expertise has plenty of fool's gold too—

fake experts who really don't know much about powerlifting or waiting tables or whatever shingle they've hung up on the Internet. That's not even including the countless scams happening online. So potential followers, fans, and members of Facebook pages and other digital portals have a reason to be wary.

Identify Gaps in Authority

Let's be honest: We may be experts, but we don't know everything, right? Even the smartest personal trainer might have skipped the chapter on the grips allowed in competitions, or even the most efficient server might not know the latest shortcut in clearing tables. These are gaps in authority, and the first step to getting over these gaps in authority is to stand before them and address the situation. Ask yourself questions such as

- Why would your industry *not* immediately give you a chance? Do you seem too young? Too old? Too busy? Too available?
- What skills are you missing?

The second step to getting over any authority gaps is to be as proactive as possible. Listen to feedback from friends, family, and even some followers about your online persona and your expert story. You can diffuse perceptions about age, availability, and experience with a few minor tweaks to your profile and your engagement.

> "Solve as specific a problem as possible," says Stirling Gardner, CEO of Stackt Digital. "People want to know you can help them with a specific issue. You will then be able to craft equally specific messaging that speaks to the fears and aspirations of your dream client. They will think you are 'in their head' and that this person 'gets me.' This will automatically help narrow you down to the go-to choice in your industry."

Let's say a financial planner named Betsy seems too young to be influencing anyone on Social Security. She could make her background as a 20-year Social Security worker more prominent, she could add client testimonials, or she could share a true story about what her parents are going through as they transition to retirement.

When Chris Tuff had the idea for *The Millennial Whisperer*, he knew a fair amount about corporate cultures and working with millennials, but he hadn't "written the book on it"—at least not yet. So he decided to write the book on it and make sure it wasn't just about him. He needed other people's stories to elevate his reputation in the leadership world. That's one reason why he also featured other people's leadership stories and included significant data from reputable, worldwide sources such as Deloitte. This let readers know that what he was talking about was supported by other business leaders as well as research. And it positioned him as being knowledgeable, connected in the business community, and dedicated to delivering helpful, research-based information.

That's what experts do. So he did what experts do. And that positioned him as an authority—as an expert—much quicker (and cheaper) than had he gone back to school for his MBA with a focus on leadership.

Getting the right data to overcome gaps in authority can take some time. "That was one of the biggest barriers," says Tuff. A great shortcut? Reaching out to people who know the data. Though he graduated from Vanderbilt University nearly 20 years ago, Chris reached out to his favorite professor who had tons of expertise in and research information on organizational development. "There was an 'aha' moment when I looked through all his data," says Tuff. "All of these things that felt like instinct to me were confirmed through the data. That moment, I thought, 'Oh my gosh, I've got something larger here.'"

So Tuff had found his Triangle of Genius, done a gut check, and started somewhat ugly, typing up his insights as free-form notes in a Google doc. Before he knew it, a book was coming together. "Developing your expert story online is similar to writing a book," says Tuff. "Instead of writing chapters, you're establishing your presence across multiple platforms that come together to create your story."

Tuff, who's also super into working out, got another motivating tip from a friend who said: "It's all about the reps, Chris, you know—reputation, man." Like doing deadlifts or squats, Tuff discovered that the more time you spend building something (in this case, a reputation rather than a fit body), the more it will pay off. "That's why you almost always say yes to being on a podcast," he says. "You're doing it because it helps you get in those reps." It took maybe 500 media interviews, says Tuff, to get over any authority gaps and firmly establish himself as an expert in managing millennials with empathy to drive profit and make an impact. "This ended up becoming much more than just the words," says Tuff.

That's true of online presence too; eventually, the words and images will give way to a more natural, free-form way of sharing information and making meaningful connections with others.

If you're missing skills that are key to your industry, how else can you acquire them? When I got serious about making a greater impact beyond the four walls of my dental practice, for example, I knew I needed more speaking experience. So I signed up for a speaking workshop with another expert— Dr. Paul Homoly, a dental treatment presentation master trainer. Pretty soon I was speaking at events like Smiles at Sea, able to confidently engage with authority.

> "We have a few clients who are type A, cutthroat, only the best for them kind of folks. It's harder to build credibility with individuals with such particular taste. Having a large following and an established reputation helps. That's only one piece of the puzzle, though. Using that following and reputation to boost those clients is what has made those relationships such positive ones. They started by saying 'prove I can trust you,' to now saying 'I need help, what should I do?' It has been a complete 360, because they know we use our influence to increase theirs."
> —**Laine Schmidt**, executive coach, Lane Smith Coaching

Disclosure and Authenticity

Successful industry influencers are also prepared to share how their background has contributed to what they are doing now, and honesty is always the best policy. I became a dentist partially because my mom had really bad teeth in her late 30s and had to get dentures at an early age.

But I really became a dentist because my sister called me a loser.

I had finished my senior year of college and went to Belize for a weeklong graduation trip that turned into six months. During that time, my sister, who'd been practicing dentistry for several years, said, "Do you want to be a loser the rest of your life?" That question hurt. Pretty soon thereafter, I found myself at Texas A&M College of Dentistry, discovering my passion for building relationships and making connections while also helping patients.

Other questions to ask yourself while writing your expert story include

- What made or makes you passionate about your desired area of expertise?
- What is your "why" and how does that relate to your story?

Remember that your followers or people you want to do business with want to know you're passionate about what you do. Maintaining a consistent voice—your natural voice—is also key to effective expert stories. Whether I post a Facebook Live or host a podcast, I'm the same exact Glenn Vo—the same Glenn Vo, in fact, who rescued himself from loserdom by becoming a dentist. (I'm not going to lie, though: Belize was a pretty awesome place to live for six months.)

Consistency is also a priority in just what you post too. A coffee expert should be posting about coffee—not how to poach salmon or fix a flat tire. A successful coffee industry influencer shares images that correlate with her story of, say, bringing her laptop every day to a local cafe to the point where she knew how to make every drink on the menu and decided to become a barista. She's found her Triangle of Genius, and now's the time to show off her expertise.

Networks and Net Worth

A friend of mine named Angie, who is an independent florist, recently set a goal to double her income within two years. She couldn't get past the beginning of her expert story: how she could get started and introduce herself as an expert.

So she sat down with her financial advisor who knew her well. Her financial advisor performed a mind-mapping exercise with her. First, she started identifying ways she could double her income as a florist or outside of her business. They came up with the following:

- Charge more.
- Work more.
- Work faster.
- Hire more people.
- Build a better network.

- Take on bigger clients.
- Teach others.
- Expand her network.
- Eliminate small projects.
- Nurture her current network.
- Create a video course.
- Speak for pay.

Then, the financial advisor asked which one would have the most impact on doubling her income. She identified speaking for pay or doing a video course. As they discussed her plan further, they realized the easiest way to achieve her goal would be to build, expand, and nurture her network. By doing so, she would open herself up for more opportunities while positioning herself as more of an expert. And when people see you as the expert you are, they're willing to pay a premium for your products or services.

Thus, building, expanding, and nurturing her network would help her achieve each of the ideas they listed. She could charge more if she built or expanded her network of customers to include higher-end events. She could work more if she expanded her network to support needs outside of her business. She could work faster if she could nurture relationships with vendors and other key people to help her work more efficiently. The list goes on.

Each way to grow her income came back to building, expanding, and nurturing her network. They realized her future net worth would have a direct relationship with her current and future network. No matter your industry, your expert story also needs an introduction, which we'll discuss in the next few chapters.

Creating Your Triangle of Genius

- Determine what gives you expertise: education, passion, experience, or all three.
- Learn more about purpose from Amy Balog at the-purposelink.com.
- Read *The Millennial Whisperer* by Chris Tuff.
- Identify your gaps in authority, and get over these gaps by connecting to outside resources and creating a game plan to learn any skills you might be lacking.
- Identify your best connections in your current network and start reaching out to them to maintain contact.
- Visit drglennvo.com to discover tools, courses, books, and more.

Chapter 3:

Examining Your Digital Footprint

As I started writing this book, movie theaters nationwide were about to debut a new fantasy thriller film, *Gretel & Hansel,* based on the Brothers Grimm fairy tale about the sweet-toothed siblings and a cannibalistic witch. It was uncanny timing because Hansel and Gretel (who did not, to my knowledge, call her brother a loser for hanging out in Belize too long like mine did ...) have been on my mind lately. Not because of all that sugar that would make a dentist shiver, but because of the trail they left behind and how it led them to get lost.

As nearly everyone who read the story as a kid will recall, Hansel and Gretel leave their home for the forest,

49

where they leave a trail of pebbles so they can find their way back. The pebbles work. But the second time they leave their home for the forest, they have no pebbles and leave breadcrumbs instead. Lo and behold, birds eat the crumbs, and the siblings get lost and discover the witch's house disguised as a candy cottage. (Spoiler alert?)

Hansel and Gretel eventually outwit and triumph over the witch, getting home safely to live happily ever after, but it's a cautionary tale about what happens when we leave the wrong trail behind us. Posting content, of course, positions us as authority figures. That's why the third step to building industry influence is to post content, with one caveat. This step isn't about posting just *any* content. Simply posting *more* content won't do the trick and can even backfire.

Creating an effective online presence to build industry influence requires creating an effective digital footprint or "trail," to borrow from Hansel and Gretel. Much like the breadcrumbs left behind by Hansel and Gretel, low-quality or redundant content will cause Google to sweep away your digital trail or footprint, leaving you far down Google's search results. And unless you're on the first page of search results for relevant terms, you might as well not exist, at least as it pertains to getting organic search traffic to your posts.

So how do you create an effective digital footprint? You consistently share quality content that details your Triangle of Genius. You share Your Natural Talents. You show your passion. And you demonstrate the need for your expertise. Here's exactly how to do that.

Detailing Your Triangle of Genius Takes Time

Before we get too deep into the steps, let me encourage you. This process takes time. While that might be discouraging, it's actually great news for two reasons. First, you will make mistakes as you detail your Triangle of Genius. Everyone does. We struggle to find our voices. We struggle to be consistent. We mess up the technical side of things. It happens. Second, you will have the fewest eyes on your content right now. Your audience will grow over time. So make your mistakes when fewer people are watching. Stay consistent and your audience will get sizeable as you master detailing your Triangle of Genius and work your way onto the first page of Google search results.

As online marketing guru Neil Patel explains on his website: "You write blog posts. You create videos. You participate in social media. And yet, *crickets*. You're *creating* content, but it's not getting you very far. Unfortunately, creating content isn't enough to really market your business.

"If no one is engaging with what you're producing, you're simply wasting time, energy, and resources to clutter an already overcrowded web."

Patel points to seven reasons why nobody might be reading your content:

1. You have no strategy.
2. You're not publishing enough.
3. You're confusing content with sales pitches.
4. You don't know your audience.
5. Your voice isn't genuine.

6. You're not promoting.
7. Your content isn't properly optimized.

We want original, consistent, and high-quality content to pave the way for our followers to find our online platforms. "It takes time to craft messaging that your audience will want to engage with," concludes Patel. Some of his examples:

- Red Bull's use of videos to show off sponsored extreme sports, drawing more than 7 million subscribers to its YouTube channel
- GoPro's high-quality, eye-catching Instagram photos
- Webinars sharing how past participants have used their skills to change their lives or careers

In the past, this messaging might have been in the form of handy tools given out as freebies at a trade show: a Swiss Army knife with your construction company's logo, for example. In the future, engaging content could take place across any number of yet-to-be-invented platforms. But no matter the medium, making an impact means taking the time for polished creativity.

Dr. Len Tau, a fellow dentist who recently wrote *Raving Patients* about online marketing and reputation, has some excellent tips on maintaining a good digital footprint. If you own a business that gets reviews, Dr. Len teaches in-depth how to make sure potential customers—your audience—get a great impression from the get-go.

While the platforms may change, the message is the same: you want a five-star online reputation.

Your Online Reputation

Here's what Dr. Len Tau writes about Google, Yelp! and Facebook in his excellent book, *Raving Patients*, which I share with his permission:

Google

As of this writing, Google accounts for 88.1% of search-engine market share. According to a ReviewTrackers 2018 survey, meanwhile, Google is the review site of choice: 63.6% of consumers say they are likely to check online reviews on Google before visiting a business—more than any other review site.

Consider also these statistics from Internet Live Stats, Statista and Blue Corona:

- 3.5 billion Google searches are made every day.
- The volume of Google searches grows by roughly 10% every year.
- Every year, somewhere between 16% and 20% of Google searches are new—they've never been searched before.
- 90% of desktop searches are done via Google.
- 60% of Google searches are done via mobile devices. Only five years ago, the figure was nearly half that—34%.
- Google captures 95% of the mobile search engine market in the U.S.

- Roughly a third of all mobile Google searches are related to location.

Meanwhile, BrightLocal's Google Reviews Study of 13,341 dentists (found using 1,799 related keywords) reveals that:

- 84% of dentists have Google reviews.
- Dentists have an average of 38 Google reviews.
- On average, dentists have 4.6 stars.

Clearly, Google reviews are essential. You must get these reviews to not only rank higher on the local map pack, but also to be relevant. For those in California who think Yelp! is all that you need, think again. Dominate Google, dominate search ranking ... repeat that three times.

Yelp!
The moment when people are looking for a business on Yelp! is at a critical point when they are ready to make a buying decision. When people are reading Yelp! reviews they are usually on the verge of becoming patients, and a couple of positive reviews could be enough to get them into your office. Patients are encouraged to write longer reviews and they normally do, sometimes with very detailed accounts of their experiences in their office.

In general, reviews on Yelp! are longer than reviews on Google. Just like on your Google My Business page, with a Yelp! business listing you can add your own content so that you have more control over the way your business is presented. Yelp! customers can add their own photos along with their reviews, but they may not always be the best images. Adding your own photos to the business listing can be a good way to tailor your brand image and make your Yelp! page look more appealing.

Yelp! is useful for website rankings and getting your business seen online. In SEO terms, Yelp! is considered an "authority" site, meaning that it can carry more weight and help boost traffic to your site. According to a 2018 study by ReviewTrackers, 45% of customers say they are likely to check Yelp! reviews before visiting a business, a percentage second only to Google. If you claim your Yelp! listing, you can add a link directly to your website, and it will boost your rankings in Google.

Facebook

Facebook isn't always the first place business owners think of when it comes to online reviews, but Facebook reviews are becoming increasingly important. No matter what demographics you're trying to reach, a significant chunk of your dream audience is on Facebook, where they're sharing recommendations with friends and perusing reviews written by strangers.

According to a 2019 study by RevLocal, about half of consumers check Facebook reviews for small businesses, and 80% of consumers are likely to choose a business with positive Facebook feedback. Ratings appear on the main menu, providing an instant snapshot of the way your patients feel about your practice.

> Searching for your business on Facebook also shows how many "likes" you have (another form of social proof).
>
> Each positive review you receive can act as unique content about your practice, writes Len. "The more you get, the more Google and other search engines see your practice as something people are interested in. So, garnering as many positive reviews on the sites that matter most allows review sites to populate page one of Google's search results and push other things—potentially negative comments—to page two, which might as well not exist."

Quality over Quantity

Are you publishing enough—or too much? It's a hotly debated question in online marketing, and the answer is often dependent on your profession. If you're a Colorado meteorologist in the middle of ski season, you're going to post at least once a day, thanks to the changing conditions. But for most people, it's generally better to pare down and avoid over-posting.

In 2000, digital marketer Dennis Yu wrote articles about why bloggers should post once a day. Twenty years later, he's cut way back, thanks to smarter search engines prizing quality over quantity. Still, when people see their traffic falling, they just post more. "Like flooring the accelerator when the emergency brake is engaged," writes Yu, "they don't realize they're making matters worse."

A much better strategy, Yu explains, comes from

- A content calendar that targets your audience. (For example, if you're a chocolatier, you'll want to post more often around Valentine's Day, Mother's Day, and Christmas.)

- A topic wheel that can help generate ideas based on how your audience responds to posts. (For example, if you're a travel writer and get lots of comments from an article on New England, the topic wheel could help spin ideas on fall foliage, clam chowder, Boston history, and more.)

- Spontaneous content production that shows you're up to speed on current events. (For example, I might notice a *New York Times* article about the price of teeth whitening and write a post on Nifty Thrifty Dentists that day about how to reduce the cost.)

5 Questions for Dennis Yu, CEO, BlitzMetrics

One of the best ways to learn is to learn from those who have gone before you. Even simple conversations with people who have built their own influence can yield priceless insights into not just what they did but also how they did it and why it mattered.

There are no better examples of building influence than Yu and few people as open as Yu about all aspects of building his business and influence. A former leader at American Airlines, among other companies, Yu is now an internationally recognized lecturer in Facebook marketing. He's also the founder of BlitzMetrics, a digital marketing company that partners with schools to train young adults. Recently, he sat down with me to answer a few questions about his company and his Triangle of Genius.

What do you see as the attraction of BlitzMetrics for potential clients?

We have something we call "repeatable excellence," which is being able to get the same result over and over. I learned this in the airline industry. We'd have weather-related delays and cancellations. The pilots and flight attendants would strike. Fuel prices would go up. There'd be a mechanical failure on an aircraft. Yet, for the most part, there were hardly any fatalities in the airline industry because of repeatable processes and checklists and systems to kick in so that we had what's called "graceful failure." Even if something goes wrong, you don't have catastrophic failure. Fine, the plane's late by five minutes, but you made it from New York to Los Angeles in five and a half hours on a trip that would have taken two or three generations on the Pioneer Trail. Think about how amazing that is. Why can't that be the same in digital marketing?

How has creating BlitzMetrics changed your business?

BlitzMetrics is like my child, my baby. I want to see it grow. I want to see other people's lives impacted. My way of immortality is to see how many other people can benefit from mentorship. We need to encourage other people to have an abundance mentality, which is based on putting in the work and training and following checklists. Thus, it's not just about business, which is about economic viability; it's about things that are worthwhile, that bring people together, that you can feel good about, that are sustainable.

What do you wish you had known before starting BlitzMetrics?

I wish I had known that the power of connection is way more powerful than that of expertise. Maybe because I was growing up in an Asian family and I went to Chinese schools and I studied really hard like the stereotypical Chinese, I thought that good grades were the most important thing. Certainly, they are important, but what was most important, that I missed and wished I spent more time on, were those connections.

I remember I wanted to be a pro athlete. I wanted to work for Nike and I applied. I did everything that a young 18-year-old thought would be necessary. I had great times. I could run a mile in 4 minutes and 35 seconds. I had really good grades. I had endorsements. I even flew out to Paris to the Louvre and took pictures of myself in front of Nike, the winged goddess of victory. And I didn't get in. But other people who were not athletes, who didn't have good grades, got into Nike because they had the connections. That made me cynical at first. Then I realized, "You know, you really do need both." If you want to make an impact, you need to have the connections because it's not who you know, it's who knows you, of course.

But it's also about having the expertise to be able to bring together both sides. You need to be able to make the connection and be able to add value through that connection, not just to know somebody. I started studying math. Studying things that I wouldn't really need to know, but I could pick up later because of search engines.

I don't regret a lot of the learning that I did because it taught me discipline. I read thousands of books. That's basically what I did until I was 30. I just read books. You can judge the quality of someone's knowledge by looking at how many books they have. If you walk into their living room, what's the dominant fixture? Is it the television or is it the books? How many books do they have?

What specific tips can you provide on increasing influence, especially for people who have time-consuming day jobs?

Increasing influence for working professionals means being known because you wouldn't be a dentist or a chiropractor or an entrepreneur unless you had some kind of expertise and passion. But 95% of the time people just don't know who you are. So, instead of going deeper into expertise, which was my mistake, make sure people can see you.

We have something called "Facebook For A Dollar A Day." It's sort of like a "day in the life" when you get to see yourself as a journalist and interviewing other people. Maybe you're at a conference and, instead of taking a picture, you ask that person a question and make a 15-second video. Things that might be obvious to you are super mind-blowing expert tips for other people. It's not about you being famous, but about you sharing knowledge because you happen to be with other people who know a lot. That's the number one way to build your influence. It's getting other people to talk about you, showing who you're with, not boasting about yourself and your lifestyle. The dollar a day strategy will change your life. It is across LinkedIn, Facebook, Twitter, YouTube. It's merely paying for exposure and letting the algorithm do the heavy lifting for you.

How do you create consistent content and why is that important?

Think of this like breathing. You're always breathing. You don't have to remind yourself to breathe. It's just like a habit. How many days does it take to build a habit? 30? 40? When you build a habit of sharing your knowledge, sharing what you care about, sharing the stories of your employees, of your patients where you're allowed to, of other people in your community, of hobbies, of something interesting that struck you, you're not trying to push an agenda. You're just trying to help other people advance against their goals. When you do that, you've built something called the Topic Wheel, which is like an onion that starts at the outside. From why, to how, to what, which is in the very center.

Good content is sharing things that are meaningful. Maybe you take a photo or video of the sunset and just say you thought about how beautiful it was. Or some interesting factoid. For example, when I go to Whole Foods, I go to the buffet and I stack it

> with meat, because it's the best thing, and it's the same price per pound. $7 a pound. Why not put meat in there instead of mashed potatoes? I'm just sharing a cool little factoid. When you do that, you build your brand. You attract the right community. Other professionals respect that. You learn how to communicate better. You get invited to speak. You can promote your book. All sorts of good things happen.

What to Post: Emotional versus Informational Posts

When posting to social media, aim for more emotional posts and fewer pure informational posts. While that might sound odd when you're looking to build a business as an expert, it's important. You can share content that's informative but do so in a way that connects with people on an emotional level. Here's what I mean by that.

Imagine you follow a marathon runner named Nicole on Facebook. She has just won a major event and her trainer is trying to decide what to post. Which of these Facebook posts would you respond to?

- "What a race! Nicole set an INSANE pace and never let go—we're all in tears here."
- "Nicole notched negative splits, running an average of 5:40 miles up until the 12-mile mark, where she kicked it up to 5:08, even squeezing some sub-5-minute miles in here."

If you picked the first one, you're onto something. Now, let's say Nicole just placed a disappointing fourth at a major event. Which of these posts would you be more likely to respond to?

- "We're all immensely proud and moved to tears by Nicole's performance. Heartbreaking, but there will always be other Olympic Trials."
- "Nicole notched negative splits, running an average of 5:40 miles up until the 12-mile mark, where she kicked it up to 5:08, even squeezing some sub-5-minute miles in here."

In this situation, either one might work, although the first one is the safer bet. That's because a study in the *Journal of Marketing*[5] found that, while emotional posts can positively affect followers regardless of a situation's outcome, informational posts had a positive impact after negative outcomes.

The researchers examined a European soccer team's Facebook page from 2011 to 2015, collecting and studying 265,530 team posts as well as user comments during and shortly after games. They found that it took just four informational posts to boost followers' feelings by 20%.

The takeaway: If you need to break any bad news, or even if there's just a lull in your news, share some information to keep your audience engaged. In all other situations, stick with emotional posts, even when you share information.

---

5   Matthijs Meire et al., "The Role of Marketer-Generated Content in Customer Engagement Marketing," *Journal of Marketing* 83, no. 6 (September 9, 2019): 21–42, https://doi.org/10.1177/0022242919873903.

Like Your Results

Also, importantly, when it comes to our digital footprints, our reputations beyond the Internet are at stake with everything we do! And, these days, our Google search results are the top indicator of our reputations.

Have you googled yourself lately? If not, open a private or incognito Internet window, google yourself, and see what you think. Private or incognito mode is important. That turns off what Google knows about you and your search history so your results will be what people are likely to see when they google you for the first time.

Do you like what you see? A study by BrandYourself.com found that 48% of people who google themselves did not like the results.

> "Reputation is important, reputation means revenue, and reputation matters." **–Dr. Len Tau**

Remember the almighty power of social media. According to a late-2019 report from the Pew Research Center, 72% of Americans use social media, and social media has now surpassed print newspapers as a news source:

- 52% get their news from Facebook.
- 28% get their news from YouTube.
- 6% even get their news from Snapchat.

With so many millions of eyes scanning these sites, who knows who might pick up our trail? These are the four main ways to leave a great digital footprint.

1. Create Multiple Social Media Profiles

The best industry influencers have profiles on all the main sites: Facebook, LinkedIn, Instagram, YouTube, etc. When someone is searching for you or your niche online, you want that person to have access to you on all the same platforms they use. We'll discuss optimizing these profiles in the next chapter.

Here's a look at my own social media profiles.

My Social Media Accounts

2. Post Quality Content

Search engines like original content and dislike repro-
duced content. In fact, they will penalize you for copying
content from elsewhere. It happens; one study found that
29% of pages had duplicate content. Or take it from Google itself:

> ### Google Search Console
>
> Duplicate content generally refers to substantive blocks of
> content within or across domains that either completely match
> other content or are appreciably similar. Mostly, this is not
> deceptive in origin. Examples of non-malicious duplicate content
> could include:
>
> - Discussion forums that can generate both regular and
>   stripped-down pages targeted at mobile devices
> - Store items shown or linked via multiple distinct URLs
> - Printer-only versions of web pages
>
> If your site contains multiple pages with largely identical content,
> there are a number of ways you can indicate your preferred URL
> to Google. (This is called "canonicalization."[6])

6   Google, "Consolidate Duplicate URLs with Canonicals | Google
     Search Central," Google Developers, accessed April 1, 2021, https://
     developers.google.com/search/docs/advanced/crawling/consolidate-
     duplicate-urls.

> However, in some cases, content is deliberately duplicated across domains in an attempt to manipulate search engine rankings or win more traffic. Deceptive practices like this can result in a poor user experience, when a visitor sees substantially the same content repeated within a set of search results.
>
> Google tries hard to index and show pages with distinct information.

So it is essential that your content is original but also has value so there are repeat visitors.

3. Maintain Consistency

You have to consistently provide content on all your social media platforms and websites. Search engines reward quality, but they also reward consistency. Having fresh content will also keep your followers engaged. For example, at NiftyThriftyDentists.com, my audience finds videos from my Facebook Live feed, which I've also converted into audio format to be listened to as a podcast. I've repurposed one mode of content into another one—an easy way to keep things fresh.

4. Create Diversity

Diversify your content so that it shows up prominently on the search engines. Also by diversifying your content, you are able to reach users in their preferred medium. Some people may like podcasts, some may like video livestreams, and some may like blogs. It's similar to watching

ABC instead of NBC back in the day or listening to an Audible book instead of checking it out of the library. By offering a diversified footprint, you will gain more followers—something I've learned firsthand by creating multiple types of media on Nifty Thrifty Dentists.

Let's take a look at Dr. Mike, an example of someone who has a good digital footprint and online presence.

Now, let's consider an example of bad digital footprints. Start with the UPS employee who was fired for allegedly posting a racially insensitive comment on Facebook. Or Roseanne Barr, whose show was canceled after she posted a racist tweet. Or James Gunn, the writer-director who was fired from *Guardians of the Galaxy* over inflammatory tweets.

You get the picture: the difference between a good digital footprint and a bad one can either elevate you or devastate you.

More on Content and Core Offers

Remember that providing free quality content on social media helps you prove your value and showcases your Triangle of Genius. So post advice and tips that showcase your expertise on your social media pages, website blogs, and within social media groups.

But avoid a common mistake up-and-coming influencers fall into: being vague. Someone will post a question or mention a struggle. They'll reply with something like "I have a three-step system that can help you. If you want to learn more info, send me a private message." Not only will that type of response get you kicked out of many social media groups for being salesy it will make you seem slimy and not helpful. Instead, be thorough and specific in your response. Be as helpful as you can. Others will see you as someone who can help with similar problems, and the person who asked the question will either look to you for more help or be more likely to reach out the next time they have a problem.

You can also ask questions to make emotional connections with your audience. Continuing the powerlifting example from chapter 2, you could post a video of someone ripping trees out of their backyard and post a question: "What do you think of John Powerlifter ripping that oak tree out of his backyard? Better than deadlifts?" If you run a deal brand like Nifty Thrifty Dentists, you could also ask your audience, "What kinds of deals would most appeal to you?"

Many followers will be looking for more custom, in-depth, or organized content. No matter how much you share on social media or even through books and other content, there's only so much content you can share effectively in each medium. Thus, it's important to pair the content you create with core offers that can offer even more help to people. Like my Side Gig Multiplier program at drglennvo.com/resources, which builds upon the lessons I share online and in this book, you can create courses, consulting offers, keynote presentations, and other content that ensures people who want to go further with you have options.

Set aside time in your schedule for creating those types of courses, consulting, and making keynote presentations. And until you have created your own, you can refer people to other experts or resources to help solve their problem. Become an affiliate of programs you believe in and you can even make money by referring people to get help from others. Your audience will trust you even more for helping them. And if another expert is a better choice for them even after you have core offers, continue to refer people to those experts. The other experts will often reciprocate, and you will build more trust with your audience.

Nifty Networking: Know Where Your Audience Is

Once you have multiple of your own quality, consistent, and content-diverse platforms, it's time to take the next step in building your influence: posting outside of your online empire. Think of online content in two buckets. The first bucket includes sites you control like your website and social media channels. These places are great for building a following and nurturing your audience. The second bucket includes websites outside of your online empire—places you don't control. These are places where new audience members hang out, such as listening to other people's podcasts, watching someone else's YouTube channel, or engaging in Facebook groups.

When I was growing the Nifty Thrifty Dentists group and started making engaging posts in other Facebook groups, for example, people naturally started following me. The same happens when I'm a guest on other people's podcasts or on an interview posted to their YouTube channel.

In Facebook groups, I'd post about getting dental discounts and deals and helping people lower the overhead in their dental practices. I also shared templates to control staff costs and spreadsheets to help organize dental supplies. I provided them for free to ultimately provide value for them and for me.

Pretty soon, a whole bunch of dentists who like saving money, and also dental companies looking for cost-cutting tips and publicity, became curious. They found my Facebook page, friended me, and found my website.

When I started doing my *Nifty Thrifty Dentists* podcast, I was able to continue to nurture these relationships and really share my personality: another dimension of my online presence. Interviewing people and genuinely connecting with them also got my name out there even more. People began to know me from my podcast.

I also started appearing on other people's podcasts, which automatically has increased my sphere of influence, thanks to the popularity of podcasts today. All that content and the images created alongside them completely reshaped my online footprint. As a result, here's what you see when you google me today:

Starting a podcast or appearing on other people's podcasts are some of the more powerful steps you can take to reshape your search results. As Nielsen and Edison research reveals, 32% of the American population now listens to podcasts at least once a month, and 94% of podcast listeners are active on at least one social media channel. Those numbers are growing too.

> Our company began in 2016, with the intent not being a company, but a small practice. That quickly changed. When word started to spread at the powerful results our clients were seeing, the demand for coaching grew. That's when the team grew, as did the services we offer. As people became more aware of our company, our reach was extended, and we were able to build more B2B relationships. With that, we saw a need for a different type of networking in our area.
>
> We began The Business Lab, a live, monthly networking event in August 2018. The first event sold out quickly, with 50 professionals in attendance. From that first meeting, The Business

> Lab has grown to a few hundred attendees, we have corporate sponsors, and a podcast that launched in 2019. What began as a desire to make a few bucks doing what I loved, is now a movement of professionals banding together to help each other thrive.
>
> **—Laine Schmidt**, Executive Coach

Share your Triangle of Genius where your audience hangs out already and you can quickly reshape your search result. And don't forget to start ugly. Once you know your natural talents, are naturally energized by your passions, and have studied industry needs, effective networking comes naturally. Get started and adjust as you go. With all the options online, you can be live and sharing your Triangle of Genius within minutes. In the past, you had to wait for trade shows or other events; today, we can post on social media immediately or start a podcast in a matter of weeks. In the future, it will happen in ways we can only imagine. The key lesson here is to know where your audience is and start sharing your Triangle of Genius with them wherever they are.

Digital footprints start with making that one first post. If it were Hansel and Gretel, it would be that first breadcrumb, but we're smarter now and know how to leave a higher-quality, longer-lasting trail. And the trail can begin where you want it to begin. You might make your first post in someone else's Facebook group. You could show up on someone else's podcast, start your own podcast, begin a blog, or film videos for YouTube. Whatever you choose, get started with that one first post and, soon enough, you'll start building momentum. Over time, that momentum will build authentic authority and influence.

Before you post, though, remember one rule—especially when posting in other people's groups or appearing on other people's podcasts or YouTube channels. Whether you're online, networking the new way, or off-line, networking the old-fashioned way, the same rules of courtesy and demeanor apply.

Take the off-line world, for example. Let's say I was joining a Rotary Club, and I wanted people to buy insurance from me. Anytime someone had an insurance question, I would chime in and be helpful. I might also make a kind offer, such as, "Guys, if you have any questions about insurance, just ask me." I'd be a helpful member, with a good reputation so more people would be willing to work with me outside of the Rotary Club. But you wouldn't hear me pitching people or giving them a hard sell.

While that might seem obvious, way too many people break that rule and wonder why nobody pays attention to them. I once had a dental rep join the Nifty Thrifty Dentists Facebook group, and all he did was sell. He provided no value and just kept posting something to the effect of "Message me if you're willing to buy this." That's all he did. I ended up kicking him out of the group and then had a long talk with him. I said, "Hey, look, people were complaining that all you did was sell to them, and all of the pitches were clogging up their feed, and they were actually leaving the group, which hurt the group." Once he could see that, he learned how to provide value. He rejoined and started providing educational posts that help other dental professionals—without promoting his company or trying to sell his services to dentists. Now, his business has grown. He sold more when he "sold" less.

The bottom line is, there will always be new versions of networking: different platforms, new social media channels, countless new opportunities. But if you keep that same rule in mind, you'll be fine wherever you go. Be respectful and avoid engaging in any negative or salesy behavior and you'll start attracting attention and, eventually, sales. Like the dental rep, you'll sell more by "selling" less.

Networking at Events

One of the many people who have given me networking advice is Elijah Desmond, the Smiles at Sea founder. "Get uncomfortable and meet new people," he says. "If you go to a networking event and you hang out and go to breakfast and dinner with the same people who you already know, you are going to expand your network zero."

My best advice for networking events: get used to hanging out late—if you're the person who goes to bed early every night, don't plan on getting a lot of networking accomplished. "Go to things that are after hours," says Desmond. "Those are where the networking actually happens, where the business happens. That's where relationships happen."

Online Etiquette: Dos and Don'ts

Do

- Go where your ideal audience hangs out and plant your flag. (This might happen off-line too: a Facebook group could be meeting for a happy hour to discuss computer coding, creating a good chance to connect with them in person about your own coding expertise.)
- Be yourself and engage with people. Be a resource to others. Be a connector. Do the things people value.
- Provide value and give freely in other groups and when you post on your profiles and in your groups.
- Consider starting your own group or circle as you grow your reputation.
- Be a positive resource, and keep your posts positive.
- Be a giver. Give 5 or 10 times more than would be expected and more often than you ask for anything.
- Become an ally of the administrators or creators of the Facebook groups you join, and follow their rules.
- Help grow other Facebook groups by being an active member and providing value.
- Build a legacy for the future. Remember that when you "overshare" or are "self-centered," your posts and content are in a group until you delete them or an admin does.

Don't

- Go into any group and attempt to commandeer the conversation.
- Try to make your ideal audience change their habits.

- **Shout (write in all caps).**
- **Post anything you would not say directly to someone in person.**
- **Overpromote.**
- **Post anything negative.**

If you don't have the time or the tech-savviness to post high-quality, consistent content, never fear: plenty of help is here, including my own training on becoming an industry influencer, which you can access at drglennvo.com/resources. (Hint: in less time than it took Hansel and Gretel to outsmart the witch, you'll learn smart ways to create and repurpose content, using an easy-to-follow schedule that will allow you to keep your day job and your sanity.)

Creating Your Triangle of Genius

- Examine your current digital footprint: What type of impression are you making? Are you duplicating content, posting inappropriate photos or words, or veering way off subject? Remove all of this low-quality or redundant content immediately.

- Build or rebuild your website and your social media profiles, establishing a presence on Facebook, LinkedIn, Instagram, and YouTube. You don't need to be everywhere, but focus on the channels where your ideal audience gathers.

- Join groups on Facebook and LinkedIn that align with your area of expertise and make your first post on one of their pages. It should be compelling enough to get people to google you.

- Seek opportunities to appear on podcasts; consider creating your own podcast and filming videos for YouTube or Facebook Live.

- Use good old-fashioned networking while online, and follow the etiquette dos and don'ts.

- At events, get uncomfortable and meet new people. Plan to go to after-hours or off-schedule get-togethers, which is where the real networking and relationships happen.

- Discover more of Neil Patel's outlook at neilpatel. com.

- Read *Raving Patients* by Dr. Len Tau.

- Learn more about Dennis Yu's work at team-blitznation.com and blitzmetrics.com.

- Visit drglennvo.com to discover tools, courses, books, and more.

Chapter 4:

Optimizing Your Online Profiles

———

"**W**ho are you?" That was the response I got when I asked the president of a local dental society if I could speak at one of its meetings.

To be fair, he followed up that comment with a smirk and a pat on the back that suggested he was joking. He also encouraged me to send an email to his assistant about my topics and my credentials at the end of our exchange. This was in 2017.

In 2018, the president of a different dental society asked me to be one of the keynote speakers at its event. I hadn't reached out to them. They reached out to me.

The difference between 2017 and 2018?

My social media presence.

That's why optimizing your online profiles is the next step to becoming an industry influencer. You picked your niche. You started sharing your expertise, your Triangle of Genius. You started ugly and began taking control of your digital footprint. Now it's time to optimize.

Thanks to my updated profiles and actions, I got the attention of the second dental society president and showcased my Triangle of Genius without even knowing he was paying attention. He had followed me on Facebook and LinkedIn, read my blogs, watched my videos, and was a fan of the podcast. He already knew my credentials because my credentials were readily accessible.

> "It's a big day in the life of an organization when you can say you work internationally. This day happened for us in October of 2019 when a global shipping company reached out to ask if we'd come in and do a team strategy session with their 12 directors. They flew in their people from countries all over the world, and we spent a day guiding them through the best ways to communicate the movement of essential cargo from one country to the next. I walked out that day and it hit me that we were a part of something that keeps the world moving. It was a great feeling. Where did they find us? Online. LinkedIn to be exact. The use of consistent marketing and brand awareness set us up for this amazing opportunity."
>
> **—Laine Schmidt**, Executive Coach

The New Business Cards

Business cards, as we all know, are becoming obsolete. According to some sources, we throw out 8 billion of the 10 billion business cards printed every year. But back in the day, whenever you met someone, you'd exchange business cards and, when the Internet took hold, conduct a little online research on each other. Today, we're researching each other even before we talk. Whenever someone connects with me online, I search through social media—Facebook and LinkedIn, primarily—and see if they have a website.

So today, your business cards are your social media profiles. People check out your profiles before they ever hire you. Make sure your social media profiles match the messaging you want people to receive from you. After all, if you're a lawyer, you wouldn't give someone a business card with a picture of you dancing on a table, would you? So don't post those pictures to your social media profiles.

It sounds simple, but things go awry when it comes to online profiles. True story: a woman we'll call Wendy is an expert in events and also runs a business helping companies book speakers. Wendy creates events for professionals who want more experience in public speaking. She provides tips, helps develop speaker pro packets, and works on websites for these individuals. She understands the power of getting in front of an audience. I heard about Wendy when I wanted to get more public speaking experience. We connected, she offered to arrange a meeting, and I searched for her on Facebook, like everyone does these days. When I found her profile, the first thing that struck me was her banner and profile photos. Her banner photo was of some mountains and her profile picture was a cat. There was really no other information about what Wendy offered to professionals. Like many in my shoes would do, I blew her off initially. It seemed like she was just a crazy cat lady who lived in the mountains.

Eventually, I messaged Wendy and scheduled a call with her. On that call, I gently suggested that she change her profile to something more professional. She said she had a different profile on LinkedIn. "But maybe some people don't look at LinkedIn," I say. "Maybe they just find people on Facebook. And if that's the case, your profile is not optimized, and if it's not optimized on every single platform, you're losing opportunities."

Another true story: a woman we'll call Beth is an expert on sleep apnea. Again, she's a great speaker and very knowledgeable. But her banner image was full of umbrellas and her profile picture was a flower. You can't tell anything about what she does, but a simple swap of photos could let people know Beth teaches about sleep apnea, as I told her. Sure enough, when she switched in images of herself speaking at one of her events, more people wanted to connect with her.

It's tricky; I get it. We want to have Facebook profiles that showcase our awesome lives, our hobbies, our passions. But if we want to have industry influence and make an impact on our businesses and others, we must forget the fluffy photos and posts—or save them for a private channel for friends and family only—and focus on posting images and words pertaining only to our expert story.

Yes, it's true that unclear or unprofessional profiles might not turn off everybody. But even in the best-case scenario, they do nothing to *help* you either. An optimized profile with professional pictures confirms people's curiosity about you and makes it much more likely that they contact you. Best-case scenario with umbrellas and cat pictures is someone doesn't get turned off. If they're actively looking for a speaker, coach, or consultant and are looking up five other experts, the much more likely scenario is they're going to be impressed with another expert's profile and lose interest in you.

Take a look at these pages gone wrong and gone right.

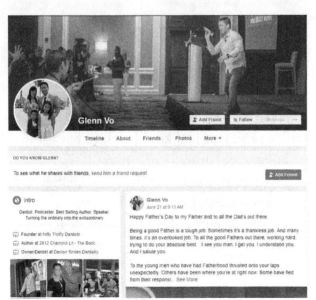

This first page is like an effective business card: polished, to the point, and consistent with brand messaging. When you share it (or when people search for you on social media), potential connections are excited and motivated to take the next step.

Now let's consider a different page.

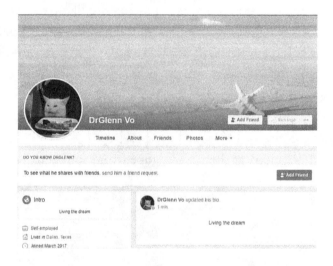

This second page is like scribbling a stick figure on a cocktail napkin: cute and kind of funny, but with no real information or opportunity to connect.

Which person would you be more confident hiring to speak to your team? After all, the person you hire will reflect on you. Who would you want your reputation to depend on?

Consistency Is Key

When you build your professional social media profiles, your work will become easier. Unlike Wendy above, make sure your profiles are consistent across all social media sites. Use the same professional images so people know they've found you.

But what about content? Because people use each social media site for different purposes, content can be completely different from one site to the next. That said, the messaging and the professionalism need to remain consistent. Just position the content for the platform it's posted on.

But what about personal profiles? Like the examples of Beth and Wendy earlier, many of us have Facebook profiles designed to show off our interests and hobbies. Many have multiple Facebook profiles, one of which looks light years away from what appears on LinkedIn. It makes sense: we want the business world to see our best sides—our accomplishments, connections, and insightful ideas—and we also want family and friends to see our best sides, which might be our backsides tanning on a Caribbean beach.

"To create a presence that raises awareness and intrigue, you must be consistent," says Laine Schmidt, the Florida-based business coach. "Consistency will come in the forms of frequency of posts, types of messaging, the aesthetic of your brand, and replying to comments." Schmidt points to the "mere exposure effect," which holds that the more we see or hear something, the more we like it. (This may not hold true for seeing a dead rabbit or listening to dubstep, but you catch the drift.)

In 1968, study author Robert Zajonc wrote in the *Journal of Personality and Social Psychology* about

1. The correlation between affective connotation of words and word frequency,
2. The effect of experimentally manipulated frequency of exposure upon the affective connotation of nonsense words and symbols,
3. The correlation between word frequency and the attitude to their referents, and
4. The effects of experimentally manipulated frequency of exposure on attitude.

"Our level of trust increases," explains Schmidt. "Being in front of our audience frequently and with a message that speaks directly to their pains or pleasures, will make our presence one they welcome."[7]

If you keep a personal profile, consider changing your name so it doesn't come up when people search for you. Still remain professional on your personal profiles but do what you can to avoid confusion when people search for you.

How Nifty Thrifty Stays Consistent and Regular

Consistency can be tricky, which I know firsthand from launching Nifty

---

7   Robert B. Zajonc, "Attitudinal Effects of Mere Exposure," *Journal of Personality and Social Psychology* 9, no. 2, Pt.2 (1968): 1–27, https://doi.org/10.1037/h0025848.

Thrifty Dentists. As I've written, it's all about saving money and getting dental deals and discounts—so people are constantly posting in my group about ways to save money and getting dental deals. I manage this on a consistent basis, so there's always fresh material. Now I've created a new health professional entrepreneur group, and I'm going to launch the *Doctor Entrepreneur Podcast*. It's the same approach: consistent content, consistent blog posts. Being consistent is a must if you want to position yourself as an authority in that particular space.

With Nifty Thrifty Dentists, I was able to grow my community to more than 33,000 members because everyone knows this is the place to get tips on saving money—and getting the newest discounts and deals that no one else can get. My community has also grown because I maintain a regular routine. So ask yourself: Are you posting once a month? Are you posting once a week? If you're only posting once a week, then why would people want to follow you? Why would people want to stay on top of that? It has to be consistent. You have to put yourself in that position. Think about it. Why do we subscribe to certain newsletters? Because they bring value to what you are looking for. And it's consistent.

> "Be yourself and you will attract the people you want to work with." **–Erin Blackwell**, photographer and owner of EB Personal Branding

Podcasts are another good example of platforms you can use to build an audience and authority. As I write, two popular ones come to mind: one from comedian Joe Rogan and another from U.S. Navy SEAL Jocko Willink, author of *Extreme Ownership*. Their podcasts are also on video, and they're posted consistently and regularly. If you want to be an industry influencer, at the minimum you need to post something new every week—every single week.

I also recently had the chance to interview Chris Krimitsos for this book. I'll share more about his advice in the next chapter. He turned Podfest Multimedia Expo from a small get-together to a huge event for the podcasting world, now attracting thousands of attendees after only six years. One piece of advice that stuck out to me from Chris was his take on consistency. "Consistent content beats out inconsistent content," says Chris. "If you don't have the luxury right now of producing content, remember that you are building an audience. Treat it like work."

Conversion-Focused Optimization

If you've ever seen a post going along the lines of "Great product. But try my new self-tanner! You can buy it right here for just $5 a tube!" then you know exactly where I'm coming from. Salesy posts are as much of a turnoff as the guy holding a giant yellow SALE sign for a mattress shop, standing there all day on the corner of Starbucks and Michael's.

There's a better way, a subtler way, to sell yourself more like the person casually mentioning in the middle of a barbecue that they just happen to be working on a product for healthier, more rejuvenated skin. You're intrigued, right? This comes down to conversion-focused optimization, which online marketing expert Neil Patel explains.

"Imagine a marketplace in ancient Rome," he writes on his website. "Let's say you're trading precious diamonds that you've managed to get a hold of from the far corners of the ancient empire. Like many other marketers, you offer your goods in a market stall. Over the course of the day, 100 toga wearers pass your stall and start trading and debating with you. Hermes, the god of trade, wants good things for you, and you convince 30 of your visitors to buy a diamond.

"The day before, you were a little sleepy, and since espresso hasn't been invented yet, you only managed to sell 15 of the valuable jewels, even though the same number of people, 100, visited your stall. However, that means that from one day to the next, you doubled your conversion rate—an increase of 100%!"

As Patel continues, the conversion rate describes the share of visitors to your website who actually buy from— or, in our case, engage with—you. "You could call it a conversion if someone who visits your Twitter profile ends up following you," he writes. "Or, a conversion could happen when someone visits a landing page that you created and signs up for your email list. In online marketing, a conversion is when your visitor takes the action that you most want them to take."

That action might be anything from buying that self-tanner to making a commitment of $100,000 to your charity. It's simply the art of subtle selling—and not really selling at all, because you're passionate about your product, and it should sell itself through your consistent, quality approach.

Your Triangle of Genius Has No Room for Bad Profiles

So what happens when part of your online presence is embarrassing, misleading, or just plain wrong? There are the completely unprofessional LinkedIn bios, such as the person who wrote this in the summary section: "To make it short, I work harder than you."

Then there are the cringeworthy Facebook pages we've all seen, full of college-partying photos showing red Solo cups or something out of *Girls Gone Wild*.

Twitter? We've all seen countless tweets that make us wish some people would shut their beaks.

Hopefully, your infractions have been mild. But either way, you can delete your bad self from the Internet with these steps I've discovered.

Problem: You google yourself and discover a photo or information that does not chime with your Triangle of Genius. Let's say my friend Dillon, for example, is working to become an influencer in the fashion industry—but stumbles across a photo of himself wearing parachute pants in the 1980s. It's a funny infraction, but some people take this stuff seriously.

Solution: You find the original source and connect directly with the site owner. Google only removes photos and information if they might lead to identity theft or are nude images posted by someone else. Your only shot to get it taken down is to ask the source. And, as always, ask nicely.

Problem: You find a photo on Facebook, Instagram, or Twitter of yourself that belongs nowhere near your business. Maybe you're working to showcase your vegan cooking, and there's an old shot of you butchering a pig.

Solution: All of these social media sites offer options to delete the photos (you can find more specific details at Digital.com). If someone else posted the photo, once again, you can find the original source and ask nicely. You can also report the problem to the social media channel. And the same goes with bad or false information: go to the original source and politely request removal.

Problem: The bad photos and information still lurk out there.

Solution: Overcome the bad with the good. You have your Triangle of Genius, remember? So channel it toward the good by following the principles outlined in this book. Post consistent, quality content, and take back your reputation by using keyword research. If you're a dog walker named John Chase, and you find positive search results when you search "John Chase," but then you combine "John Chase" with "dog walker" and find a photo of yourself walking down the middle of the street with a bunch of leashless, snarling canines, it's time to take back that keyword. You can do this by using "dog walker" in all of the positive content you create.

Why Facebook Works for Showcasing Your Triangle of Genius

Facebook is one of the biggest social media platforms around. And, although some people think a lot of "old" people are on Facebook, don't let that deter you. The "older" crowd might be your audience. You have to look at who your audience is and where they hang out. Maybe your audience is on Instagram where they just want to look at images and quick posts. Maybe your audience is on TikTok. Maybe they're on Clubhouse. Or maybe they hang out at trade shows. Be where they are. But, for most people, Facebook is a great place to start. Why?

Facebook works. Many industry professionals have Facebook profiles. And while it might not be the coolest place in the world, people still visit Facebook every day. Even better, Facebook is designed to be influencer-friendly because it allows you to create a business profile where you can put out consistent content for free. You can even boost your reach for just a few dollars using its ad platform.

You can create a personal brand right on Facebook. I have my personal profile, Glenn Vo, and I have my business profile, Dr. Glenn Vo. I also have my different groups: Nifty Thrifty Dentists and Healthcare Professional Entrepreneur.

On my personal page, I can adjust the settings to post photos and news for the public to see or read, or I can make them private. I can create different audiences. I don't want the whole world seeing pictures of my kids, so I keep those private.

Remember, we all know that the first thing people do whenever they meet somebody or read something about them is look them up—they search Google, Facebook, and elsewhere. And you can control what they see by setting up professional profiles and optimizing them.

When people look me up, I want to show them a highlight reel of what I want them to think of me. I want people to think of me as an entrepreneur, an author, an industry influencer. So some posts I make public. And I also like to disclose that I'm a Christian. It really means a lot to me. I want people to see that I'm writing a book. I want people to see that I care about the community. That is the power of Facebook.

If you have people following your Facebook pages, you actually can run ads targeted toward your followers. So let's say you have a course or a speaking engagement. You can use the power of Facebook to run ads so your audience can see what you're doing.

Whether it's Facebook, Instagram, LinkedIn, TikTok, or Clubhouse, your audience is out there. And there's always a new site popping up. Keep your eye out for those new places and be there if your audience is. Identify where your audience is. Then market your content to them.

> "Having a strong presence on social media is how you'll establish the personality of your brand, whether personal or professional. People pick up on consistent themes in your messaging. Even if

you weren't intentional with what and how you were posting, those themes will naturally occur. This is why intentionality is vital. Your brand's voice will be out there, loud and clear for the world to hear. What do you want it to say? Is it consistent with your end objective? One of the greatest benefits of a strong online presence is awareness. Social media is a funny animal; sometimes it leads to quick results, and sometimes people use it as a way to watch you … for years, until they are ready to make a move. Your online presence gives people a window into what you do and why you do it. What a great opportunity for you to make known to the world the value that you offer." —Laine Schmidt, Executive Coach

Your Triangle of Genius Can Start the New "CD of the Month Club" for Less Than a Penny!

Phil Collins, Wham!, Madonna—these were just a few of the '80s bands some of us listened to on repeat (using an actual level to rewind) thanks to the Tape of the Month Club from Columbia House. It took WAY longer to listen to these artists, of course, than today when the Internet instantly spits out any song ever recorded. Others of us got to enjoy They Might Be Giants and Soul Coughing with the CD of the Month Club. But the principle behind these monthly deals is the same: you choose a bunch of options for a penny. Then, they send you more music, which you have to buy. This is called negative option billing, which is actually a positive option for your Triangle of Genius. It's about giving away free products in order to entice an audience. Only, because you're becoming an amazing industry influencer making a huge impact on your community, your audience will be more than happy to pay for your services, whether it's your online presence they can follow for free or a speaking engagement that charges a fee.

Creating Your Triangle of Genius

- Remember that quality content is crucial for your branding and image.
- Create content to attract the right audience—you're better off with 600 ideal followers than 6,000 random followers.
- Create Facebook Live videos.
- Keep quality blog posts on your website.
- Develop lists, documents, and tools to help solve a problem or grow the business.
- Engage with your audience.
- Learn more about Laine Schmidt at laineschmidt.com.
- Delete social media photos with tips from digital.com.
- Read *48 Days to the Work (and Life) You Love* by Dan Miller.
- For more tips on optimizing your online presence, check out drglennvo.com.

Chapter 5:

Expanding Your Expertise and Influence

———

There are plenty of rock stars in the podcasting industry. But if we were drafting podcasting influencers to watch over the next decade, my first pick in the draft would be Chris Krimitsos, whose Triangle of Genius is connecting people through the power of podcasts.

As I mentioned in the last chapter, Chris founded Podfest, which is an amazing conference for new and veteran podcasters covering everything from creating and launching to monetizing and marketing a podcast. His strengths include facilitating events—he has facilitated more than 2,000 of them for the group Tampa Bay Business Owners alone, which he founded in 2008. His passions include listening, evaluating, and effecting change. The podcasting industry provided plenty of opportunities to listen, evaluate, and effect change. And when it comes to industry need, Chris's ability to see the bigger picture and connect podcasters with each other has filled a big need in the podcasting world—independent podcasters needing access to community and opportunities. Ta-da—Triangle of Genius.

A consummate learner, Chris is a prime example of someone who is always expanding his expertise and influence. From hosting dinners to posting content, he just gets it. We'll draw on some of his tips in this chapter as well as explore other ways to remain actively engaged with our audiences. These tips will help you take the next step in cementing your position as an expert: expanding your expertise and influence.

What Is Your Intent?

This point in the process of building industry influence is a good time to revisit your intent in becoming an industry influencer. That's because we can get so focused on the content creation, social media sharing, and other steps involved in becoming an industry influencer at this point that we lose a little bit of the spark that led us to start in the first place.

Whether your spark came from this book or some other place, take a few minutes to remind yourself why you wanted to become an industry influencer in the first place. What impact did you want to make? What personal freedoms did you want to unlock? What family goals will becoming an industry influencer help you achieve? Remind yourself of these on a regular basis to keep your flame burning bright.

Maybe you're still getting ready to take the first steps. That's fine. Still remind yourself of the reasons you want to achieve them and keep those reasons top of mind at all times. No matter what, your "why" will always be your guiding light (and get you out of bed when it's cold outside).

"You want to leave an impact on your industry and leave it better than you found it," says Krimitsos. "So intent needs to be clear. When you have clarity on your intent, your 'Why' becomes bigger than the fear of 'How.' And when your 'Why' becomes bigger than the fear of 'How,' you're off to the races. It doesn't matter if you're a podcaster; you could be a really great guest on other podcasts. But to be a key person of influence, you need a methodology."

With your "why" top of mind, let's get back to all the ways you can expand your expertise and influence as you build your reputation as an expert.

E-Introductions

Chris is constantly introducing people to each other, even when he's not at Podfest or other events in person. "I'll start introducing my peers and becoming a person of record as a connector, bringing them together," he says. His work stays consistent regardless of where he is.

One of the best ways to get e-introductions for you is to make e-introductions for others. Know two people who would benefit from knowing each other? Reach out to each of them and ask if they want an introduction. Then make those introductions by email or social media direct messages. Even offering those connections will get you top of mind in people's minds and generate an urge to reciprocate with mutually beneficial introductions for you too.

Dinners

If you're attending a conference, plan ahead to host a small networking dinner. "Pick 12 people you know are going to be at the event, including a couple of friends," he suggests. "If you don't have the budget, make it breakfast or lunch." Kick off the meal by clearly stating your intent and going beyond the "I'm glad you're here" opening. "It sucks when no one states the intent, because I'm sitting there eating dinner thinking, *Why am I here? Am I going to meet anyone?*" says Krimitsos.

Instead, try opening up the dinner by saying something like this: "My intent is for us to have an amazing time and create relationships that will last us a lifetime as we help our patients and ourselves in this journey called dentistry." Then give each person 10 seconds for their name, where they're from, and the focus of their practices. "When you say 10 seconds, this does something unique," says Krimitsos.

"It takes the fear off of giving an elevator speech, especially for people who don't like speaking publicly." During those 10 seconds, it's your job, as the facilitator, to listen for an interesting tidbit you can use to connect the people at the table—which will change the energy in the room. "Now everybody's gonna start sharing with everybody else."

Or ask participants to turn to their left and tell the craziest patient or client story they have. "People always bond over these common pain points, especially when you're in a niche business," says Krimitsos. "Innovative opportunities will start to come across your desk before anybody else's by hosting these dinners. Information is power, and knowing something is going to happen is very powerful. You can make money; you can do something for charity; you can help your community. Plus, you could be the person who gives it the stamp of approval, and everybody else will jump on it only after you've tested it."

> "When you have clarity on your intent, your 'Why' becomes bigger than the fear of 'How.' And when your 'Why' becomes bigger than the fear of 'How,' you're off to the races."
> —Chris Krimitsos, founder of Podfest Multimedia Expo and producer of *The Messengers: A Podcast Documentary.*

Networking Never Stops

Whether you're at an event, sending follow-up emails, or posting content on your and others' sites, staying engaged with your audience is key to expanding your expertise and influence. When I started networking with other dental professionals, I quickly learned how valuable and rewarding it can be if you network consistently. Networking changed my life, and I've witnessed countless other professionals improve their lives too. Here are three benefits I've found from networking with other dentists within my industry.

You Can Share Resources

My brand is called Nifty Thrifty Dentists for a reason. I like saving money and helping other dentists save money too. When I network with other dentists, we can share resources or deals on supplies and can even join together for group-buying deals.

In the Nifty Thrifty Dentists Facebook group, we can share dental forms, practice documents, vendor connections, and more. The more we share, the more value we add to each other.

You Can Get Mentored—and *Be* a Mentor

Learning, being open to learning, and being willing to share wisdom from your experiences are three of the most important traits to develop if you want to rise to the top of your industry.

No matter how much experience you have, you won't know everything about everything. Even less experienced people in your industry will have more knowledge and expertise on *something* than you. You can learn *something* (usually many things) from everyone in your industry. And they can learn from you. Even professionals who are just starting out will have a totally new outlook that can freshen up their business. Professionals who have been in the industry for decades can share wisdom from common experiences. You can even learn from businesses in different parts of the country or world. I guarantee there isn't a single person in your industry from whom you can't learn *something* (even sometimes what *not* to do). That's why it's important to approach networking with an open mind and as an opportunity to share what you know and learn what others know.

You Can Connect with Some of the Most Generous People in the World

Professionals who network regularly are very generous people. They understand the value of helping others and, as a result, are constantly helping each other. I have consistently been blown away by the generosity of dental professionals. Whether it is one professional helping another with advice or direction or a full-scale giving event where vendors and practice owners donate supplies or other resources to each other. That generosity is contagious and inspiring.

While you might not think that generosity extends to your particular niche, you'd be surprised what happens when you simply put your best self out there and lead with a generous, helpful approach to networking.

Relationship Building Expands Your Influence

Julie Stoian builds relationships better than almost anyone I know. Former stay-at-home mom turned funnel builder, copywriter, agency owner, and now co-owner of the seven-figure company, Funnel Gorgeous, Julie builds and leverages relationships to impact more people every year.

She's a great example of someone with influence who seeks to make an impact.

Julie's proven her marketing and relationship-building expertise many times, but one particularly notable instance is her first big affiliate promotion for a Pete Vargas product launch. Although she was fairly unknown at the time, she had built such a strong relationship with Pete Vargas, himself, that he promoted her to his audience alongside such big influencers as Tony Robbins and Michael Hyatt.

A Great Relationship Sets the Foundation for Higher Sales

Julie's generosity and relationship-building approach to marketing didn't only score her points with Pete Vargas; it also built deep relationships with her own audience. Her audience loves her. *Adores her*, really. In the world of online marketing, she brings a refreshing approach to her audience. Unlike many online marketing experts, who tout their profits and luxurious lifestyle, Julie stays down to earth and is a straight shooter. And when she launches a product, she gives to her audience generously through unexpected bonuses, extra live calls, and adding more value into a single $37 course than most influencers pack into $1,000-plus programs.

Not only do they *love* her they also *trust* her. So if Julie says something is good, they know that it will be. If Julie says she trusts someone, her audience knows that they can too. If Julie says she'll give a certain bonus, her audience knows that not only is she true to her word but also chances are she'll offer even *more* than she promised.

Her generosity and strong relationships paid off for both Julie and Pete, landing Julie fifth out of the many affiliates for Pete Vargas's launch, many with much larger audiences than Julie's.

A Great Relationship Sets the Foundation for More Exposure

While Julie's relationship-building impacted her bottom line on Pete's affiliate promotion, the bigger impact for her business came from the connections she gained with other affiliates and people in Pete's audience, many of whom previously weren't aware of her. That has led to more opportunities for Julie, including landing a main stage at a major conference.

A Great Relationship Does the Legwork for You

Because Julie built a great relationship with her audience, her reputation precedes her. Any new member of her free Facebook group, new customer, or even new acquaintance knows that she's a woman of her word and consistently offers high value with everything she does.

That reputation makes it much easier for her to sell her products and services. Unlike many marketers who have to convince buyers they can help them, Julie's audience takes much less selling. She receives less resistance, has to do less legwork to get a new customer, and needs to do less convincing that what she provides will help—all because her audience already knows the quality of person she is and the quality of the product she provides.

Consistently networking and adding value can do the same for you too. This will come in very handy as you expand your expertise and influence in other places. And one of the best next steps to take when you get to this point in your influence-building is to start a podcast.

Creating a Podcast

Once, it was called audio blogging. Today, it's called podcasting, and it's truly taken off in the world of industry influence. Although it might seem that everyone has a podcast these days, compared to other platforms, there's much less competition for attention in the podcasting world.

As of March 2021, there were almost 2 million podcasts, according to the latest research,[8] and the number is climbing almost daily. While that might seem like a lot of podcasts, compared to the number of blogs or social media accounts, it's merely a fraction. For example, according to GrowthBadger, there are more than 600 million blogs as of March 2021.[9]

More than 50% of Americans have listened to a podcast on topics ranging from Sasquatch sightings to snacking on Premium saltine crackers. Trust me, the podcasting world has room for you and your Triangle of Genius.

---

8   Ross Winn, "2019 Podcast Stats & Facts (New Research from Apr 2019)," Podcast Insights, April 11, 2019, https://www.podcastinsights.com/podcast-statistics/.

9   Kyle Byers, "How Many Blogs Are There? (and 141 Other Blogging Stats)," GrowthBadger, January 2, 2019, https://growthbadger.com/blog-stats/.

"If you're an expert in a certain field and you want to talk to your fellow peers, then I would definitely recommend looking into podcasting," says Podfest founder Chris Krimitsos, who has a few step-by-step instructions:

1. Search Apple Podcasts for podcasts related to your area of expertise.
2. Click on a show that looks relevant to you and what you're looking to build.
3. Scroll down to the section called *You Might Also Like*. Then click *See All* to see what shows Apple Podcasts suggests.
4. Notice what keywords appear in the titles and descriptions for each of those shows.
5. Plan to incorporate some of those keywords into your show title and descriptions, because they mean your potential audience is searching those words and looking for more content.
6. Don't worry about how many other podcasts there are related to your area of expertise. "When you see a lot of choices in a niche, that's actually a good sign," says Chris, explaining that it indicates a healthy interest in the topic.

Some of my other favorite questions for generating a new podcast include the following:

1. What's Your Podcast For?

- To generate leads for a business?
- To be recognized as a leader in an industry?

- To share an important message?
- A networking tool to meet influential people?
- To have fun?

2. Who's Your Podcast For?

- Other people in your industry?
- Potential leads and clients?
- Other like-minded individuals that you can create strategic alliances with?

3. Why Should They Listen?

- Does it satisfy the needs of your audience?
- Does it provide value to your audience—whether that be entertainment, education, or inspiration?

> "I grew up in Oyster Bay, New York, about a mile from where Teddy Roosevelt was buried. There's an inscription there: 'Keep your eyes on the stars and your feet on the ground.' Couple that with my philosophy of 'start ugly,' and you can accomplish anything you want. Just be willing to fail. Label failure as just trying different things, and then label them a success."
> —**Chris Krimitsos**, Podfest founder

Industry Influence Endures: Examples

Expanding your expertise and influence needs a check-in every so often. Ask yourself the following questions again:

- Do I have something important to say?

- Do I have something important to share with my industry?
- Do I want to impact more people than those within the four walls of my business?

Surveys have shown that 60% of consumers look at online reviews weekly, and 93% of consumers say online reviews impact their purchasing decisions.[10] I know that's enough proof for me to see how my posts and videos can impact my industry.

Checking out the work of some industry influencers can also boost your motivation. For me, the best might be Tom Bilyeu of Impact Theory and Pastor Steven Furtick.

As Tom's website explains: "Impact Theory's mission is to pull people out of the Matrix, at scale, by giving them an empowering mindset. We do that by creating the best-in-class entertainment and educational content." Basically, Tom interviews other influential people, and this entertaining and educational content is consistent across the board, from his website and YouTube channel to his Facebook page, where he has more than 1 million followers. The graphics are sharp, and the message of empowering mindsets is clear. That's empowered Tom to interview everyone from skateboarder Tony Hawk and author Rachel Hollis to rapper Chamillionaire and icon Deepak Chopra. Sure

---

10   Laurie Fullerton, "Online Reviews Impact Purchasing Decisions for over 93% of Consumers, Report Suggests," The Drum (March 27, 2017), https://www.thedrum.com/news/2017/03/27/online-reviews-impact-purchasing-decisions-over-93-consumers-report-suggests.

this is Tom's full-time job, but it's more evidence of how impactful industry influence can be.

> "Know your customer," says Suzanne Edwards, founder and CEO of AlphaMamas Fitness. "Know their hurts and desires and needs. But mostly know their wants. Why do they want the solution? The want very often trumps the need."

Then there's Pastor Steven Furtick. Based in Charlotte, North Carolina, Pastor Furtick reaches people around the globe thanks to YouTube, where more than 1 million subscribers can see him speak on topics including managing the pressure to measure up, being your own cheerleader, and finding your joy (which all also happen to be particularly relevant to many of us managing side gigs).

So exploring some success stories out there can boost your confidence, as can revisiting your Triangle of Genius. If you're feeling stuck in any of the three points, you can begin to identify the cause. Chances are your talents will only get better (which I discuss more in-depth below), but are you still passionate about powerlifting or brewing beer or teaching others to needlepoint? Perhaps you've discovered the industry no longer needs another person presenting ideas about plant-based protein. No problem. The beauty of online influence is that you can restart if necessary.

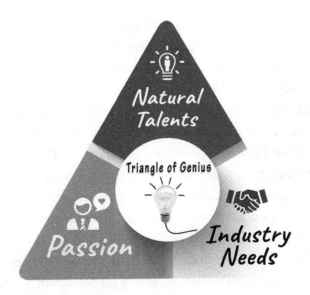

Expanding Your Expertise

Back in the day, expanding expertise was just called "learning," and we did it by "reading a book." Today, we can become better at our Genius Ability through courses, YouTube videos, Facebook group discussions, and many other of the same online resources we already know how to use—and in more ways than you think.

Take Tom Bilyeu, for example. He could invite Annaka Harris on his show *Impact Theory* to learn and share knowledge about how to challenge everything with his audience. I might invite a dental coach on my podcast or to the Nifty Thrifty Dentists Facebook group. Like Tom, both I and my audience would learn from that experience. In doing so, Tom and I would be learning more about our areas of expertise—while increasing our industry influence.

Even better, our guests will likely tell their followers to check out the episodes too. That allows us to grow our audiences even more. In this case, sharing your audience generously with other experts who can help them causes the tide to rise for everyone—the expert, your audience, and you. If someone is looking for Facebook marketing advice, for example, I'll often send them to Dr. Anissa Holmes, even though I know quite a bit about Facebook marketing. If I think she can serve them better than I can, I refer the person to her. If someone is looking to have a great continuing medical education event, especially on a cruise ship, I'll direct them to Elijah Desmond at Smiles at Sea, even though I've hosted several events myself. Being selective with my time to focus exactly on my Triangle of Genius and referring people to other experts also helps me expand my expertise and influence even deeper, without distracting myself from my best focus by something that I'm only pretty good at.

The learning opportunities are endless. It gives me goosebumps just to think about it. Be selective with your time by focusing on your Triangle of Genius and you can efficiently and effectively grow your audience and expand your expertise. And remember to stay consistent with your content.

Whether you do it yourself or outsource content creation to a pro, make sure you stay consistent. That consistency keeps you top of mind in a helpful way and gives you more opportunities to connect with other influencers and experts like Annaka Harris or Anissa Holmes. I recommend choosing one type of content that you love to create and hiring someone to repurpose it into other forms. For example, if you're comfortable recording videos, create video content and have someone scrape the audio into a podcast and create articles and social media posts from your videos. If you're comfortable creating audio content, start a podcast and have someone create video, social, and article content from it. The opportunities are endless.

If you're using social media as a business, everything that you should be doing in social media should be geared toward growing your audience and growing your business wherever your audience hangs out.

3 Signs You're Building Your Industry Influence

1. You're getting more followers.
2. Your website is getting more traffic.
3. People are reaching out to you, inviting you on their podcasts and to speak at events.

Expanding Your Influence

Expanding your expertise will naturally expand your influence, especially if you network with other influencers like I suggest. In addition to that process, consider expanding your influence to be a continual process. Whether your goal is to reach 5,000 followers, 50,000 fans, or even just to build a Facebook group of a few hundred dedicated community members, influence is a finely honed tool that should be regularly sharpened.

Dr. Shawn Dill is an excellent example of someone who's *constantly* expanding his influence. The CEO of The Specific Chiropractic Centers and a practicing clinician, Shawn's a highly sought-after speaker and coach. He's also the co-author of *None of Your Business: A Winning Approach to Turn Service Providers into Entrepreneurs*, the founder of the mastermind and podcast *Black Diamond Club*, and the creator of a social media channel for chiropractors.

After Shawn graduated from chiropractic college, he moved to Costa Rica, where he practiced for eight years, with fortuitous enough timing and expertise to write the country's chiropractic regulation law. Shawn built his practice to 250 patient visits a day—in only one of his four offices. He was learning the life of a small business and entrepreneurship.

As I was finishing writing this book, I hosted Shawn Dill on my own podcast and learned what goes into a background like that and how to use it to your advantage.

"But I then had this realization that with everything that we were doing, we were really making a very small and potentially insignificant impact globally," he said, explaining his epiphany that "the world's most skilled service provides, be it clinicians, but also artists, hair stylists—anybody who's providing a service, the world's best—they live in relative obscurity simply because they refuse to embrace the idea of being an entrepreneur."

That was the impetus for *None of Your Business* and also a key part of Shawn's philosophy as he expands his influence. Here are his top tips for readers looking to share their Triangle of Genius, impact the world, and look beyond their own industry to innovate.

- Think outside of the profession you're in. Shawn brings up the fact that fast-food restaurants took the drive-through concept from banking. Now, banks rely more on ATM machines and online transactions, while having a drive-through lane is critical for fast-food restaurants looking to stay competitive.

- Consider hiring a coach. "Having a coach gives you leverage," says Shawn. "The way to get somewhere faster is through having a smart person guide another person. Coaching is allowing me to cut the learning curve and get to my destination fast."

Creating Your Triangle of Genius

- Reevaluate your intent.
- Look beyond your industry to innovate.
- Consider hiring a coach.
- Take advantage of conferences, and host your own small networking dinners.
- Network, network, network: you can share resources, get mentored, be a mentor, and connect with some of the most generous people in the world.
- Keep learning, and keep staying consistent with your content.
- Discover lessons from Tom Bilyeu at impacttheory.com.

- Get inspired by Pastor Steven Furtick at stevenfurtick.com.
- Learn the art of business from Dr. Shawn Dill at shawndill.com.
- Visit drglennvo.com to discover tools, courses, books, and more.

Chapter 6:

Where Do We Go from Here?

Erin Isaac is a pediatric dentist. But she's also much more than that. Her story could inspire *anyone* to discover their Triangle of Genius, become an industry influencer, and make an impact on their community, their family, and themselves. When Erin felt inspired to expand her professional impact beyond her practice, she took action in a big way. She loved her practice but wanted to expand her impact on the pediatric dentistry world, so she created a better online presence, a podcast, and more. Her secret ingredient: consistency.

Erin had no idea what steps to take in order to motivate and influence other pediatric dentists and other healthcare providers who take care of kids. She just knew she wanted to achieve that noble goal. So, like all of the most successful industry influencers I've come across, she looked for help in the form of a coach. As she began taking action, she approached me for some help.

When we first started working together, we kept it simple, following six simple steps to go from interest to impact as an industry influencer. She had the interest. All she needed to do was take action. To help her get started, I walked her through the action steps in this simple drawing.

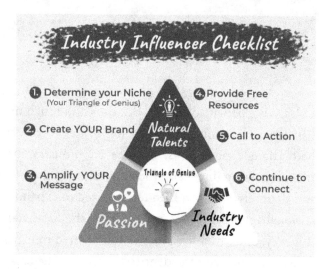

I suggested that Erin spend some time researching social media pages of other people she admires in the pediatric community. She already had created her own social media pages, so she only needed to tweak those and maintain consistency. But she didn't have a website, so she would eventually need to put one together.

At first, however, I suggested she focus on the lowest-hanging fruit, which was to optimize her social media accounts, including her private Facebook group. Adding high-quality images and a Facebook banner that delivered the right message to her audience didn't take very long. She was ready for the next step.

Step by step, Erin began to build industry influence. She recorded Facebook Live videos about pediatric medicine, COVID-19, and other topics, all along increasing her vision for what she could achieve for pediatric medicine. She started interviewing health care workers about coronavirus and other topics and inviting them into her Facebook group to generate even more momentum.

And we helped her create even more velocity by inviting industry professionals on Zoom calls and posting the call recordings to her group. Her audience loved those conversations.

As she grew, we were careful to maintain authenticity and stay true to her vision. We also continuously revisited the three steps in activating a Triangle of Genius to make sure every step we took enhanced her Triangle of Genius and helped her grow as an industry influencer:

1. Determine your niche.
2. Create your brand.
3. Amplify your message.

We made sure everything she did was true to her niche, enhanced her brand, and amplified her and her message.

And, today, Erin is continuing to build and expand her influence in the pediatric medicine world.

Erin's story is just one real-life example of how to build industry influence. So many possibilities open up when you take the time to discover, create, and promote your Triangle of Genius. It gives me goosebumps to think about the positive impacts we can all make on our communities by channeling our passions, our strengths, and the industry's needs. So where do we go from here? Everywhere.

The best way to do all of that is to keep authenticity front and center as you grow.

It can be easy to look at what other people are doing and become a copycat, thinking, "If it worked for them, it can work for me." But while that can be helpful to building momentum, it won't necessarily build something *you* love. That's why I suggest looking at what other people have done but then asking yourself, "What can I learn from that to help me?" instead of "How can I take those same steps?"

That's the only way to build an impact as an industry influencer in a way that is sustainable and fires you up. The secret ingredient to sustained success is authenticity. Always be authentic. Always be yourself.

Here are a few more examples of people who used the principles of industry influence to find a new niche or pivot within a struggling industry.

Evolving with Your Audience

As host of *The Bert Show*, a nationally syndicated weekday morning entertainment and news radio show, Bert Weiss finds himself in an interesting place, professionally. He's a member of the Georgia Radio Hall of Fame and, by any measure, a tremendous success story in the radio world. But the radio world is fading, with people's attention split between satellite radio, podcasting, and other forms of entertainment. Despite this fading industry, Bert's show has continued to grow, with his show's podcast adding millions of listens a month to his radio ratings. Between social media, podcasting, and his radio show, Bert's voice is as loud as ever, unlike many radio hosts who didn't have the same ability to pivot while staying true to their Triangle of Genius. I sat down with Bert to talk about how he was able to not just maintain but also grow his influence in the radio world—and even expand into the podcasting world, while other radio hosts have repeatedly failed.

"We're all in the connection business," he says. "I learned a long time ago that there are a million audio products on the market. We have countless radio shows and podcasts. But really what separates one from the other is the connection that you make with people. And the thing that separates *The Bert Show* from other shows that come and go is our ability to make real connections with our audiences through authenticity, transparency, and vulnerability. We don't turn on the mics and pretend we're perfect or above anyone else. We bring our true selves to the show every morning. Our audience can feel that authenticity and is drawn to it."

While many people think that it's easy for Bert to say that, having been in the business for decades. But that misses the point. Remember the principle of starting ugly, from Chris Krimitsos? That's exactly what Bert did when he first got into radio. "We didn't have any idea what we were doing. Zero. We got started and figured it out as we went."

What did that look like? First, they didn't stick to the same old radio format of saying silly things and making goofy sound effects. Instead, they just started talking. "Saying you're gonna be vulnerable and doing it are two completely different things. Many shows will say they're going to be vulnerable and authentic and then revert back to old radio habits the second the mics are on. Very few shows are willing to show their ugliness on the air. But we do and that's what connects us to our audience."

That focus on building a connection with his audience also made Bert really study his audience more than many other shows. Some hosts are still doing the same show they were doing decades ago. Bert constantly evolves his by staying current with his audience, watching their habits, and learning how they've been changing. "You have to evolve with your audience," he says. "You have to keep your fingers on the pulse of what's going on with them and then cater to it. Bring your authentic self to the world in which your audience lives. That helps you grow and evolve together with your audience."

> "There's an aspect of industry influence that requires learning to listen. Asking the right questions and just stepping back and listening instead of jumping in right away." **—Alex Molden**, leadership and development speaker and coach and host of *The Shark Effect* podcast.

Don't Compare Your Backstage to Somebody Else's Front Stage

You know your brand has landed when your website is just your first name—which is just the case with Jevonnah "Lady J" Ellison. Lady J runs a business that includes coaching, a mastermind group, and live events, including the Thrive Summit and The Entrepreneurial First Lady summit. But she wasn't always building a business. Years ago, she was still finding her way, like many people. But in just a few years, she was able to build a thriving business helping people discover their true selves and building lives of their dreams.

Jevonnah was kind enough to share her tips with me about taking your brand to the next level.

"Courage is not the absence of fear—it's feeling the fear and doing it anyway," she says of nudging your brand out there. "Get all the tools. Get all the resources. But at the end of the day, make sure you launch. Version 1.0 is always better than Version 'Never-point-0.'"

Jevonnah is also always networking and attending events to make her business stand out. "You remain a constant student," says Jevonnah, who regularly listens to podcasts, takes courses, and reads books to grow her knowledge and impact—anything to stay one step ahead of her audience so she can inspire them. She has her own staff ("I'm a big believer in hiring help," says Jevonnah), but for those who don't have the budget or the desire to hire people, making true connections with like-minded people is key to keeping the momentum going. "It's really helped my brand to always be connecting with people," she says. "And we're continuing to evolve. You can't say, 'We're all good; I'm going to sit on a beach for the rest of the year.'"

Finally, Jevonnah adds: "Don't compare your back-stage to somebody else's front stage. Anybody can put up a fancy Instagram or Facebook post. Anybody can have a nice looking website with so many plug-ins. But what matters is that the results you delivered for other people in your experience. And be authentic, be you."

> "We were born to be connected."
> —Amy Balog, executive coach and facilitator, ConnexionPoint Services LLC

Design Thinking

According to the Interaction Design Foundation, "Design thinking is a non-linear, iterative process that teams use to understand users, challenge assumptions, redefine problems and create innovative solutions to prototype and test. Involving five phases—Empathize,

Define, Ideate, Prototype and Test—it is most useful to tackle problems that are ill-defined or unknown."[11]

When building my online course, one of the subject matters that I got most excited about is design thinking. Design thinking has taken hold among countless industry influencers since Stanford professors Bill Burnett and Dave Evans wrote *Designing Your Life: How to Build a Well-Lived, Joyful Life*. It's a powerful way of thinking if you want to really build connection and influence with an audience because it makes you focus on building connections with and solving problems for an audience you want to serve.

Like Burnett and Evans did with their book, the concept of design thinking could take up an entire book or course in and of itself. But even the basics of design thinking can help you make even more progress as an industry influencer. That's because, as the Pareto Principle suggests, with many outcomes about 80% of your results will come from 20% of your efforts. In other words, if you know the 20% of the efforts that can get you 80% of the results, you can make a big impact without a lot of effort. So, I invited Eugene Korsunskiy, a disciple of Burnett and Evans and now a professor of engineering at Dartmouth College, to share his suggestions on what aspiring industry influencers should learn about design thinking to get started.

---

11 Teo Yu Siang, "What Is Design Thinking?," The Interaction Design Foundation (2009), https://www.interaction-design.org/literature/topics/design-thinking.

"Design thinking is about two basic things: mindsets and tools," explains Korsunskiy. "Designers take on cognitive dispositions such as bias to action embracing experimentation, curiosity, optimism, empathy, and collaborating across lots of different differences. These are all the mental habits of a designer. Then you also have a specific set of tools and methods and techniques. Together with mindsets, they are a really helpful framework by which to guide creative action."

As Korsunskiy suggests, when a designer faces an open-ended problem, they build empathy for the people they're designing for. That empathy allows the designer to design better solutions.

Applying that type of thinking to building industry influence, consider your future audience to be the people you are looking to help. You will build influence if you help your audience solve problems. The more problems you help them solve, the more influence you will build. But, like Korsunskiy suggests, influencers come from a place with unique experiences and biases and need to embrace experimentation, curiosity, optimism, empathy, and collaboration to better understand and serve their desired audience. This allows us to build empathy with our audience. And that empathy allows us to build authentic relationships with them.

But it's not just our audience that we need to empathize with. We also need to understand and build empathy for ourselves in order to discover our Triangle of Genius and build industry influence in a way that fires us up.

The mindset of approaching ourselves and our audience with an authentic desire to learn and help will give you the opportunity to build a sustainable business as an industry influencer.

If you haven't done so while discovering your Triangle of Genius, now is the time to start learning everything you can about yourself and your audience. Reflection, journaling, even quiet time can all help. Pay attention to how you think, how you feel, what makes you tick, and what your curiosities are as you learn about yourself and dream about your ideal future as an industry influencer.

Korsunskiy also emphasized that, as you brainstorm about yourself and your audience, quantity is a prerequisite for quality. "In brainstorming an idea, generally designers lower their inhibition," says Korsunskiy. "They stretch their imagination. They allow themselves to consider options that are silly or impractical. Then you are way more likely to bring back from that place, back to reality, some idea that is novel, interesting, creative, innovative, and one that you wouldn't have been able to have before."

Nobody's Perfect

Whether you're an A-type personality or a Z-type, it's easy for perfectionism to set in when you're growing your brand. Sure, we want our social media profiles to be sharp and professional, but that doesn't mean we should lose sleep because we remembered in the middle of the night that an element was missing.

As business, relationship, and mindset coach Tommy Breedlove writes in his *Wall Street Journal* and *USA Today* best-selling book, *Legendary: A Simple Playbook for Building and Living a Legendary Life, and Being Remembered as a Legend*, perfectionism is a killer:

"Whether setting a goal, moving in a new direction, or making a big decision, it's natural for doubt and fear to seep into our thinking. Also, for us ambitious types, we are always on a relentless pursuit of this unattainable thing called perfection. Perfection kills our ability to take our first giant step toward anything new or better, to continue to take action after starting, and even worse, to finish!

"We've spent our entire lives as high achievers wanting to be in the game, competing, winning, and eventually conquering. What happens if we fall short and are less than—well, you guessed it—perfect? Sadly, a lot of us never get started, or we quit, or, worse, stop just short of finishing our goal."

Remember, All Platforms Are Not Created Equal

Where we go from here also depends on how social media platforms will evolve over time. But some advice from executive coach Laine Schmidt helps us navigate the uncharted waters ahead. "If you're just starting to build your brand on social media, get to know the platforms," she says. "They are not created equal. They have different audiences and different languages. To save yourself time and stress, find the ones that fit your brand and your goals and invest there."

Schmidt reminds us to post frequently, build relationships, and always be studying those particular platforms. "Metrics will be your best friend," she says. "Every month, take stock of which posts are getting the most engagement and on which platforms. Replicate what works."

Look at who's engaging with you—are they your core audience? If yes, double down and keep at it. If no, you might be on the wrong platform, or you need to do some more specific targeting. "Again, you have to identify why you are using your social media," says Schmidt. "Give it a purpose. This way, you'll be able to gauge whether or not your social media strategy is working. The best way to find what works for you is to plan well, post often, and measure your results. Be patient. Allow for fluidity at first. Your social game will ebb and flow over time, but you'll find your groove."

Prioritize

These amazing influencers added another key element to industry influence once they discovered their Triangle of Genius: prioritizing. It's not a novel concept. But it's a powerful one. It's so powerful, his simple ability to prioritize is one of the many lasting legacies of President Eisenhower, a man who served as president of the United States from 1953 to 1961. As James Clear, author of *Atomic Habits: An Easy & Proven Way to Build Good Habits & Break Bad Ones*, writes: "Eisenhower had an incredible ability to sustain his productivity not just for weeks or months, but for decades."

Decades of productivity? Anybody growing their brand would happily take that. The Eisenhower Box, as it's come to be known, helps people take action with four possibilities. (I love this, as it ties back to my love of video games and the choices.)

The possibilities are

- Urgent and important (things to do immediately)
- Important, but not urgent (things to schedule to do later)
- Urgent, but not important (things you will delegate to someone else)
- Neither urgent nor important (things that you will eliminate)

My Eisenhower Box might look something like this:

What goes in which quadrant of each box? That's up to you and your Triangle of Genius. What might be urgent to one person (answering texts) is the last thing on another person's mind. And what one person might eliminate (going to the gym) might be the most urgent and important thing in somebody else's day. For more tips, you can check out drglennvo.com/blog.

How to Go Far

As you move forward in building your industry influence, remember the African proverb: "If you want to go fast, go alone. If you want to go far, go together." I love that proverb. It applies to any industry, any time, and anybody who's ready to make a long-lasting impact on their community. More than ever, our time is valuable, so investing in a team that can help you go far is a pretty smart choice, don't you think? I've put together a comprehensive course for us to go on this journey together at drglennvo.com/courses.

You can do this. Let's get going on your Triangle of Genius.

Creating Your Triangle of Genius

- Determine your niche, create your brand, and amplify your message.
- Be authentic. Be yourself.
- Evolve with your audience.
- Listen to Bert Weiss at thebertshow.com.
- Learn more about Jevonnah Ellison at jevonnah. com.

- Learn about Julie Stoian and her industry influence at juliestoian.com.
- Consider reading
  » *Designing Your Life* by Bill Burnett and Dave Evans
  » *Legendary* by Tommy Breedlove
  » *Atomic Habits* by James Clear
- Visit drglennvo.com to discover tools, courses, books, and more.

Learn the Art of Using Social Media Groups to Grow Your Business and Industry Influence

One of my favorite courses to introduce to people looking to become industry influencers is called "Groupologie: the Art of Using Social Media Groups to Grow Your Business." It's a part of my Side Gig Multiplier program that you can find at drglennvo.com/resources. I can't think of a better epilogue to this book than a quick overview of how you'll cement your industry influencer status by signing up for these classes.

As I've mentioned, I've created a group of more than 30,000 dental professionals who helped grow my brand, create a networking space, and bring in a second income stream for me. They've gotten my name out there.

Now, you can do the same through Groupologie, which covers:

- Mindset
- Making money
- Your Triangle of Genius
- How to set up a social media group
- Branding

- Increasing engagement
- Growing your group
- Getting companies to work with you

Discover this course, and much more, including my complete Side Gig Multiplier program, at drglennvo.com/resources.

Acknowledgments

First and foremost, I want to thank my Lord and Savior Jesus Christ, with whom all things are possible. "Be strong and courageous. Do not be afraid or terrified because of them, for the LORD your God goes with you; he will never leave you nor forsake you" (Deuteronomy 31:6 NIV).

Thank you to my wife, Susan, for always believing in me and for accepting me for who I really am—flaws and all. Your love and devotion to our family inspires me every day to be the best possible husband and father I can be. My day starts and ends with me thinking of you—always.

Thank you to my kids, Kylie and Jackson, for all the laughs, hugs, and kisses. And for the very important reminder that my most important job is to always be their dad.

Thank you to my mother for the unconditional love that only a mother can show her child. And thank you, Mom, for the many years of sacrifice you showed our family so that we can all pursue our dreams. Thank you to my father for giving me the opportunity to have a better life in America.

Thank you to my sisters, Brittany and An, for always "having my back." No matter what was going on in my life, whether it be good or bad, your support for me never wavered. Both of you are true examples of what strong women should be.

Thank you to my Father-in-law Danh Tran and Mother-in-law Susie Tran for always supporting our family. And to my Brothers-in-laws Steve and Michael for treating me like their own brother.

Thank you to my mentors Dennis Yu, Dan Miller, Dr. Eric Roman, Julie Stoian, Dr. Chris Steven Villanueva, Chris Tuff, Tommy Breedlove, Dr. Shawn Dill, Dr. Anissa Holmes, Eric Siu, Dr. Len Tau, and Mark Lack. Good mentors help make you a better version of yourself and not a replica of themselves.

Thank you to Dr. Hieu Nguyen, Dr. Christopher Hoffpauir, and Elijah Desmond for your unwavering support and continued friendship. I am blessed to have the very best friends in the world.

Thank you to David Hancock and the entire Morgan James Publishing team. You help make this dream a reality, and I look forward to many more collaborations in the future.

Thank you to Nick and Sarah for your help editing the manuscript. Your guidance and attention to detail helped make the writing so much easier!

And finally, a huge thank you to any family member, friend, colleague, or classmate I've had the privilege to meet during life's journey. Just know that you had a huge part in shaping my life, and for that I am eternally grateful.

About the Author

D
r. Glenn Vo is a thought leader in dentistry, a frequent speaker at national events, and a full-time dentist in Texas. He founded Nifty Thrifty Dentists to help dental professionals save money by negotiating discounts with the dental industry. The social network now has more than 30,000 members while Glenn's podcast has been downloaded more than 1 million times.

From an early age while growing up in Pasadena, Texas, Glenn was a natural at building authentic relationships. He had plenty of flair as a waiter for TGI Fridays and also used his sales skills to melt diners' hearts into ordering extra cheese fondue at The Melting Pot. Dentistry, however, is his true profession. After attending the Baylor College of Dentistry for his dental training, he later co-founded Denton Smiles Dentistry in Denton, Texas, with his wife, Susan Tran, in 2009.

Glenn realized while growing Denton Smiles that fellow private practitioners were missing out on deals from corporate dentistry, and he has since leveled the playing field through Nifty Thrifty Dentists. This experience also taught him the power of online promotion, which Glenn used to attract interest in his *USA Today* best-selling book, *2612 Cherryhill Lane*. It also led to his second book, *Industry Influencer*, which guides readers through the steps of growing their brand through meaningful engagement and connection online. Glenn is an active member of the Christian community. He has been inspired to funnel his passions for connection, writing, and making an impact into diverse projects.

When he's not writing books or helping patients, followers, and readers smile, Glenn's smiling along with his wife and their two young children at their home in the Dallas–Fort Worth area.

A free ebook edition is available with the purchase of this book.

To claim your free ebook edition:

1. Visit MorganJamesBOGO.com
2. Sign your name CLEARLY in the space
3. Complete the form and submit a photo of the entire copyright page
4. You or your friend can download the ebook to your preferred device

A **FREE** ebook edition is available for you or a friend with the purchase of this print book.

CLEARLY SIGN YOUR NAME ABOVE

Instructions to claim your free ebook edition:
1. Visit MorganJamesBOGO.com
2. Sign your name CLEARLY in the space above
3. Complete the form and submit a photo of this entire page
4. You or your friend can download the ebook to your preferred device

Print & Digital Together Forever.

Snap a photo

Free ebook

Read anywhere